LUCKY ME

WALKING AWAY FROM A GASLIGHTING COVERT NARCISSIST

TORI WAGNER

Lies don't end relationships
the truth does.

—Shannon L. Alder

CONTENTS

This book is for the silent, the voiceless,
the ones who no longer know who they are.
You are not alone.

INTRODUCTION

I grew up with divorce around me. Aunts and uncles, my mom and dad, my best friend's parents. I was used to it.

And I hated it.

I hated the contempt I could feel from each of my parents. And I hated the sadness, loneliness, and shame that I felt as a result. It was my norm, but I never felt normal.

At fifteen, I made a vow to myself and to God that I would never ever get divorced. There was no way I would have kids and put them through any of the ugly feelings I grew up wrestling with. I was determined to have an amazing marriage.

From the outside, I could make my life appear like an episode of *Leave It to Beaver*. I had learned how to keep up appearances no matter what I was feeling on the inside. I was smart and likable. I stayed involved in activities. I just stayed busy. And guarded. Always, always guarded.

I wanted to be known, truly known ... because how amazing does it feel to be seen by another person?

But what if that other person can read you like a book and knows exactly what to say to soften your guard? What if they are so good at reading you that you let down your guard before you know who you're letting in?

That's how it happens. You meet this person and you're like, *Wow. He sees me. He wants to know me.*

Oh, honey. He sees you. He picked you. You are everything he wants. You are everything he needs.

You are his target ... and you don't even know it. He's *that good* at disguising what he's doing to you.

But, guess what? He draws you in so completely that you have no idea what is happening because you've given him your heart *and your mind.* It's literally like a non-hostile takeover.

Lucky you. You snagged the most amazing person on the planet.

But did you?

I sure thought I had. I remember telling my parents that his character was so strong ... I'm actually embarrassed to tell you what I said. Umm. I told my mom he had more character in his pinky finger than anybody I knew.

Yes. I really said that. And I sincerely believed it.

I didn't know that twenty years later I would be searching for a place to stay in the middle of night with all of my kids just so we could get away from the man who swindled me out of my heart and was a master at mental subterfuge.

These pages are the raw reality of the life I've lived. The moments that drew me in, the ways I was sucked in again and again, how it affected my faith and mental headspace, how I reached for help that escaped my grasp, and what it looked like when I finally walked away.

You're about to learn what happens in the heart and mind of a woman who once had spotlights shining in her eyes, how drastically the spotlight changed in the course of an abusive marriage, and what made her stay.

It isn't pretty. But it's true. And my prayer is that you'll gain a deeper understanding, learn something about yourself or someone you know in a similar situation, and by the time you read the last pages, *you'll have hope.*

Hope beyond the heartache.
Hope outside the hurt.
Hope in the healing.

LITTLE DID YOU KNOW

You get used to it.

The feeling in the pit of your stomach that shakes … that won't settle. The feeling that puts a death grip on your body and has your heart in a stranglehold. Every speck of moisture leaves your mouth.

And you hide. You hide within your own skin. The you that exists deep inside makes its way to a shallow grave.

It wasn't always this way.

One day, you're young and naive, deeply craving connection. You wake, you work, you walk through your daily life ignorant of an intimate relationship. Your knowledge of relationships and romance is gained through viewing hours of romantic television, binging *Poldark, Bridgerton,* and *Downton Abbey.* Your ideal man has been created through pages and pages written by the Bronte sisters, Jane Austen, and Nicholas Sparks.

He is charming ... Boy is he ever.so.charming.

You are invited to a friend's house. There will be other young singles. *Well, thank God for that. Maybe you'll meet somebody—finally.* Time to look cute.

You choose your clothes carefully. You want to be noticed, but you don't want to look like you're trying too hard. You take extra time on your hair and makeup. You listen to music, and a little flame of hope dances in your heart.

Several cars are in the drive when you pull up. Nerves make you more anxious than you'd like. Without realizing it, you're holding your breath a little. Just before you knock, a quick breath rushes past your lips.

Here we go.

Walking in, you quickly take in the room, searching for faces you know, taking care not to hold eye contact. *Look pleasant ... look ... approachable. Yes, approachable.*

You casually duck out of the room and find a place for your coat. Then you head for your next venue of safety—the food and drinks. A full plate means busy hands and a busy mouth. It's hard to look insecure while casually eating food and drinking from a plastic cup with your name written in Sharpie.

"Hey."

Wha-? Is he talking to me?

Your eyes leave your plate just long enough to realize he is, in fact, speaking to you.

"Hi," you hear yourself saying.

"I'm Matt. I don't think we've met," says this sandy-haired, slate-blue-eyed boy standing in front of you.

He's casual and easy. That only seems to make you more nervous.

"No, I don't think so. I'm Joy. Nice to meet you," you reply and try to focus on the plate in front of you, hoping he won't notice your completely encompassing awkwardness.

He's chewing. You're chewing. And he just keeps talking. He actually seems to want to stay right here. *He is cute. I don't even know what he's saying because I'm lost in the possibility that someone that looks like him is standing next to me. It's been so long since I've been noticed by someone I actually want to look at me.*

"Where are you from?" you hear him say, followed by more questions all about you.

You talked for the next two hours and before he left he asked for your number so he could call you.

Dear God … Is this what it feels like to meet someone who truly wants to know me? Is this how it all begins …

Yes. That is exactly how it begins. It begins in what feels like mystery and magic, the stuff of dreams. It begins with feeling like you are experiencing something perfectly precious.

You drink it all in. And you focus on the man he tells you he wants to be. The dreams he has about marriage and having a wife he'll treat like a queen. The dreams he has about being a father who dotes on his children. As he describes his future self to you, you realize he is describing the kind of man you never knew you wanted so deeply.

You pray that you can marry him. You pray for God to make him love you. He has to love you.

You don't know that in three years you'll go in your closet to cry alone and hide.

You don't know that in twenty years you will still lay in the fetal position inside of your closet to sob quietly.

You don't know that *you* will be lost.

You don't know that the sound of your own voice will become foreign to you.

You don't know that you won't be able to form sentences without fear taking your tongue under its control.

So, you beg for God to make him yours.

Little did you know.

You Are Not Okay

Several years into the relationship and I had definitely found my groove. I knew my place.

I knew that it was my job to look for ways to make him happy.
It was my job to get up in the middle of the night with the kids. NO.
It was my privilege.
It was my job to have the house cleaned up by mid-afternoon every day and before bed each night.
It was my job to keep my body slim.
It was my job to keep up with his schedule.
It was my job to discipline the kids in the style he deemed appropriate.
It was my job to speak when spoken to.
It was my job to ignore the kids when he was talking.

It was my job to make our groceries stretch every month by clipping coupons for hours and grocery shopping for four hours.

It was my job to protect him.

It was my job to respond attentively when he let me know he wanted sex by slapping my butt.

It was my job to be respectful.

It was my job to be supportive at all times.

It was my job to pretend his rage never happened.

It was my job to teach our children to be quiet and act like nothing happened … and to never speak about it, never confront, never tell the truth.

And yet … I could do almost nothing right. At least not consistently. We could not go more than a few weeks before he would rage at me because I had done something to cause it, of course.

I was never to discuss our private life with people he didn't trust. And do you know who he trusted? Well, umm … pretty much nobody.

I was doing my freaking job. And I was doing it alone.

When you are living with a covert narcissist who gaslights you, you are meant to do it alone. After all, you are not okay.

You are so far from okay. You don't even earn a passing grade. Let's see … if you were to grade yourself based on what he has communicated to you it would probably look something like this:

Housekeeping: D (You never keep all the crap cleaned up, and there are dishes in the sink every day.)

Respectfulness: D (If you respected him more, he would show you more love. But you don't know how to be respectful in the right way.)

Parenting: B- (You feed the kids every single day, but you are not good at disciplining them.)

Hygiene: B (You don't always shower before bed, and you don't keep your legs shaved.)

Submissiveness: D (You do not submit to his leadership appropriately.)

Organization: C (You keep up with his schedule, but you do not keep the house organized.)

Godliness: C (You are unable to recognize your own sin, so he has to point it out to you.)

Intimacy: F (You never want to initiate sex. It would be great if you wanted to more often.)

Your list may be different from this one. But you get what I am telling you. Do you see why you are not okay?

You are not okay because you can't be okay. Okay would mean good enough. Okay would mean you measured up. But you don't.

You are living with a yardstick that you've never actually seen. It's there. Ohhh, you know it's there. But it changes. And you have no clue what the changes are.

When a change has happened you are keenly aware because you have to hear all about how you missed the mark. You missed the mark that he tells you he has explained over and over. He is so disappointed and disgusted. He has every right to be angry with you for not doing what he has requested.

That's what spouses do, right? They make requests of each other in polite tones.

"Please wipe the counters down every time you use them."

"Please wipe the sinks and toilets every day."

"Please change the clothes from the washer to the dryer immediately."

"Come here."

"Bring me some water."

"Put away your laundry."

"Listen to me while I complain to you about my job every day."

"Please don't complain, you bring a negative mood to the house."

I could go on for days. And days. The "polite" requests were endless. Do you know how many requests I made that were received? I can't even tell you because he knew how to make requests the right way.

And I didn't.

I didn't know how to politely, respectfully, and kindly ask things. So my requests would turn into instruction time and a lesson on how I should have asked if I wanted him to respond better.

Yess. Yessss. Nothing makes a woman feel more loved and heard than a man correcting her. And that woman feels especially loved when she meticulously measured her words before they left her lips and those words were critiqued and rejected.

You are not okay. He will not let you be okay.

I was never okay. My friends would try to tell me. My family would try to tell me. But their words could not measure up against his words. His words were heavy. His words were chains on my soul.

It's amazing how well you learn to function wearing chains.

I dressed up in those chains every day and dragged them everywhere I went. And if I happened to shed them when I was away from home, he would call or text and they took up residence on my shoulders once again.

I didn't realize that I had basically given him permission to place every link of that chain around the spirit inside of me. With every contemptuous look, every snide remark, every helpful lesson about my behavior—a new link was added to my shackles.

Some of the links are heavier. Some of them would dig right in, clinging to my heart. Some of them I would feel immediately and try to shrug them off, but I couldn't.

Can You Feel Your Chains?

Your mind reels as you try to blend his words into your own when you explain away your behavior to your family and friends who ask questions. They want you to visit. They want you to have a girls' night.

As a good wife, you have to represent him well. That is what a good wife does. She builds his reputation.

So, you imagine what you can say to your family and friends that won't make him angry. What reason can you give to say no? You can't tell them the truth.

You can't say that you don't want to go to girls' night because the kids don't want to be alone with him. You can't tell them you don't want to come home to a pissed off husband.

You can't tell your family that the reason you're not driving to visit them is because he has to work and thinks it looks bad for you to go without him. Or that even though he could afford to go golfing with his buddies, you can't spend the money on food and gas to get there and back.

No. You wouldn't dare say that.

You know that if you even give a hint of disagreement in your answer, he will know. He will tell you how you made him out to be the bad guy because you always make him the bad guy.

With every excuse, every lie you tell to protect his reputation … to protect yourself from the repercussions of disappointing him … you acquiesce to wearing chains.

Gaslighting wraps chains around *your* sense of truth and shackles you to *his version* of truth.

Can you feel those chains? Can you feel the weight of him on your shoulders, your heart, in the pit of your stomach? The heavy, heavy ache in the depths of your soul weeping for rescue.

You cannot shrug off chains. You cannot violently rage and shake them off. They'll still be there after all that wrestling. Can a dog shake off its leash?

And that's what you have become. You are his dog. You get to keep him warm, listen to his troubles, fetch whatever balls he throws, and sleep in the kennel he's made for you. Obedience gets you a little pat on the head. Disobedience or disappointment gets you the boot of his disgust.

Not even well-loved dogs live on chains.

Are you okay with that? Are you okay being his dog?

No. You are not okay. You have to do something about it. Shrugging and shaking will never work.

Gaslighting is meant to keep you spinning mentally and emotionally, it's meant to keep you guessing and questioning yourself. Being off balance is the norm for you, but that doesn't make it okay.

You cannot remove chains that you refuse to see. Take a deep breath. Prepare yourself for painful honesty and guttural grief. Now look at your life.

The links of those chains have burrowed themselves into you. Each one needs to be removed. For every piece pulled away, your eyes will see more clearly and the voice inside your head will become your own again.

To Be Known

It's only two months into your relationship and he already seems to know you so well. He studies you. He asks so many questions … It's as if he knows your thoughts better than you know your own.

And his ideas. He has so many ideas about how relationships should be. He wants to keep you safe. He wants to protect you.

One morning you open your front door to find a note with a rose sitting on your doorstep. It's from him. He has driven across town while it was still dark out to deliver a love note for you to see first thing. Your heart melts. It melts deeper into his. You melt deeper into him.

You talk on the phone for hours every night. He has so many ideas. He knows what he wants and has reasons and purpose for all of it.

Wow. He is heading in a great direction. He is already being a leader.

His ideas are different from your own, but they seem to have more logic, more reasoning. He has developed his ideas and speaks them with complete certainty and authority. You tell yourself this is how it is supposed to be. This is how older women tell you it should be. And don't they all know better than you?

Your trust in him grows. Your belief in his wisdom and leadership grows.

And you are completely oblivious to the doubt that has grown in you. You don't realize you have replaced your thoughts with his. You have begun replacing the truth as *you* have known it with the truth as *he* knows it … until what you have believed about yourself is becoming hazy, what you have believed about God and life seems inadequate, and the reality of your life is no longer acceptable.

You are no longer your own. You have given your *self* to him.

And so it begins.

You have been subtly led to no longer trust yourself, to no longer believe your own thoughts or feelings are reliable. You must trust and rely on *him* to gauge your own mind.

Sure, it feels a bit wrong. But you trust him. He cares about you. He wants what is best for you.

This is the beginning.

You are immersed now. You can no longer see on your own. You have convinced yourself that he can see life better than you. He can see more clearly than you.

You are in the middle of being gaslighted. You don't know it, and you wouldn't believe it even if you were told.

The burial of You has begun.

He's not holding the shovel, *you are*. You picked that shovel up and began carrying it everywhere. It became part of you. You trust that shovel because you trust him.

I trusted him. *Me.* I carried the shovel. And if I had no shovel, I could dig my own grave with my bare hands.

Am I too sensitive?

That's what I started asking myself when I didn't feel secure … when I felt upset about something that he told me was nothing to be upset about.

I started explaining scenarios to single friends my age to get their opinion. (Excellent idea. Ask somebody else with no wisdom in this area.)

We'd been dating for several months and he was going to dinner with a friend from out of town. A female friend from high school to be exact. I didn't understand why I shouldn't meet her and I let him know.

He insisted it wasn't a big deal. He downplayed my feelings and made sure to let me know that I was making a big deal out of nothing.

So, I invited my friend to lunch and asked her, "Am I being too sensitive about this? Should I be upset?"

And, you know what? She told me no. She told me she completely understood where he was coming from.

Nevermind the fact that we had been dating exclusively for several months.

He must be more level-headed than I am. He must be more emotionally mature than I am.

That was all it took. I started tucking my feelings away into a tiny little pocket of mistrust. And I began to rely on his feelings as my gauge.

So, I begin ...

Apologizing.

After all, I was being ridiculous. My feelings were too big. My thoughts were irrational. He was the one who knew better. He was the one who made more sense.

I must be wrong. So, I apologize for overreacting. He goes out with his friend. And I stay home and ignore my feelings.

I become better and better at apologizing for just being ridiculous. I've never been in a relationship like this before. I've never been in a relationship with someone who cared about me so much that he was willing to work out all of these conflicts. So many conflicts.

And so many of those conflicts were my fault. I was just wrong.

I was wrong a lot.

I mean … I had to be wrong because his side always had a better argument. His side made more sense. I was just overly emotional and carrying too much baggage.

Right?

God was just showing me all the ways I could be a better person. Of course that must be a good thing.

Here's the reality. In the beginning, you find yourself happy. You are intoxicated by this new relationship. You are breathing him in. He has become your world. You have told your family about him. Bragged about him. Talked of his character and how wonderful he has made you feel.

Your family is so happy for you. They have never seen you so committed to anyone. They are right. You are fully committed to him.

So when he tells you about previous relationships, it's hard to hear. When he tells you about his heartbreak from the girl who loved him so desperately, you are jealous.

Yep. Jealous.

You see … I was jealous. *Who was this girl? What was it about her that captivated his heart?*

I listened as he told me that she was deceptive. How she used "I love you" to manipulate him. I could not imagine how he had to continually put her in her place. She sounded so mentally unstable.

And yet … he had been under her spell. *He loved her.*

He made sure that I knew this.

He did not tell me that he loved me, and he wouldn't. He would never give his love to anybody else until he was going to marry her. This made complete sense to him. He was honoring God in this.

He had reasons and logic behind all of his choices. So, when he talked about his roommates, how messy and inconsiderate they were, it made perfect sense. They weren't respecting him. The space they shared should be kept clean. The refrigerator should be organized. They should be doing their dishes.

It all made sense. It all sounded reasonable. It is no wonder that he was so irritated about it.

Gaslighting another person requires groundwork to be laid.

During the first stage of gaslighting, *you* are in love. You believe in *him*. You see *his* potential. You see your potential together. You imagine your future together. It's exciting. It's hopeful. *You* are all about *him*.

He is holding back his feelings because you are not married. It's his way of honoring and respecting you and God. He is leading you. He is leading your relationship.

Self-talk is in high gear.

And *is this not what you have wanted? Is this not what you have prayed for?* You have waited for so long to be known, to be led by a strong man. This must be your answer. He is your answer to years of praying.

So, you know it's up to you to be patient.

You are fully immersed in the gaslighting groundwork.

Meeting You Where You Are

You may be reading this and feeling stupid. You may be reading this and find yourself shaking your head. Shame is a wicked, wicked thing.

When you realize that the person you're supposed to trust has been gaslighting you for years, it can completely knock the wind out of you. And it can absolutely make you feel like an idiot for not realizing what's been happening to you.

I want you to know that there is no timeline for separating yourself from a gaslighting narcissist. Some people recognize what's happening to them fairly soon. Some people don't realize how bad it is for twenty or thirty years. And some people never do a thing about it.

It took me over twenty years to wake up. Twenty years!

I watched my kids being shamed and accused for years. I went months and months without hearing the words "I love you." We were all witnesses to countless fits of rage.

And I still stayed.

Shame is that hand that holds you under the water and keeps pushing you down every time you need a breath. It tells you to stay right where you are, that you don't deserve to be anywhere else but held down.

That isn't true. You don't deserve to sit in shame. Not ever. I still can't believe that an A-average college graduate who has spent hours on stage in the spotlight allowed myself to be treated that way.

But now I know my worth. I intentionally work to believe the positive truth about myself and to see others clearly. You can do this, too.

COMMITMENT

I was committed, body and soul, within a few months. I knew I wanted to marry him.

I never believed I was an easy catch. I had never *ever* been an easy catch. Every other guy may have gotten three dates out of me. After three dates, they were too clingy, too excited. *They didn't even know me yet. What exactly were they clinging to?*

It was easy. I was busy. I had a full life. Dating and committing to a relationship was not on my agenda.

Only one of them had ever held my attention. He was the one who let me just *be*. I knew Jeff liked me. I knew he was pretty enamored with me. And yet, he was never clingy.

Jeff was kind and thoughtful, witty and smart. We even loved hanging out with his parents. For months, the relationship was just easy. Honestly, it stayed easy. I broke his heart when I told him that I would be moving away.

I was never attached to Jeff. I cared for him. I still care for him. But I never loved him. Saying goodbye was not fun, but it was not hard. We had different values. I always knew it couldn't be long term.

So, when I did fall in love, it seemed like a long time coming. It caught me off guard. I didn't know what to expect. I didn't know how I would feel, act, or think. To say the least, I was unprepared.

But I didn't know that.

So, my experiences seemed completely normal and healthy. I had always been told that I was wise beyond my years. Lord knows I had seen plenty of examples that were dysfunctional.

Based on the fact that I had a knack for learning from other people's mistakes, I truly thought I knew what bad relationships looked like. And to a certain extent, I did.

My parents had both been married multiple times. Twenty-five years after their divorce they still struggled to be civil. I had made a vow as a teenager that I would never get a divorce. If that meant I would be single for my entire life, then so be it.

Because I was going to follow God.

I was going to have a Christ-centered marriage. I was going to have a marriage that would last. My children would never suffer because of a broken marriage. Nooo. Not ever. Not me. My word was my bond! (Bring on the tribal drums and loud claps of thunder!!)

Not that I had made a dramatic teenage vow, or anything.

Dramatic, or not. I was pretty darn serious about that vow. I believed it was my parents' divorce that had caused the depth of pain in my soul. That is what so much of the world had taught me. *Blame the divorce.* Blame. Blame. Blame.

Blame is a saboteur to growth.

Blame blinds you. Blame holds you captive. Blame cripples you. Blame is a habit.

You cannot see the truth when blame is clouding your vision.

You cannot move forward when blame has its grip on you.

Blaming others, blaming yourself, will not change your circumstances.

Blaming yourself for things you have no control over might give you something to cling to when you're looking for a reason why he isn't as committed as you are. Surely you've done something wrong. He will be fully committed when it's the right time.

Right?

And after the trainwreck I had seen, it was easy to believe that somebody would take their time committing to me. It only made sense that I should be patient. Plus, I had already put my trust in him. I had already decided that *his* was the voice of reason.

I committed myself to our relationship, and he knew it. He seemed to find it endearing that I was so committed, that he was the one to win my heart.

It was amazing until it wasn't. It was amazing until I was too much.

We'd been dating six months when I was headed out of town for a trip. He had decided that we didn't need to talk on the phone during that time. "Absence makes the heart grow fonder," he told me.

I did not agree. I liked talking on the phone every day. I wanted to hear his voice. I wanted to feel connected every day. There was a part of me that really believed I needed him.

Needing someone was a new experience for me. And he had a way of getting me to admit my deepest feelings. I told him that I felt a need to be with him, to talk to him … His response was to ask me questions.

He was great at questions. It made me believe that he truly wanted to know me, to understand me.

He never said he had any need for me.

Because he didn't. Not really.

My commitment to him with no returned commitment only served to entangle my feelings further. The push-pull of it all was creating a tether with knots throughout it. They were knots I was unable to untie … because I didn't even know they were there.

Knot after knot was forming. Unbeknownst to me, every one of them was sitting in my blindspot. But … Is it a blindspot if you never actually looked?

Lord knows, I wasn't looking. I had my eyes set in one direction. And my glasses were a perfect shade of rose.

My eyes were firmly fixed on him, and his eyes were on me … and my flaws.

As we watched the Olympics one evening, I commented on a girl's very odd pigtails and chuckled. My comment was met with immediate disapproval and shame. "My family would never say anything like that.

My sisters would never speak so unkindly about another person ..."
and on and on. And on.

I was in tears.

I was completely taken aback by his contempt. He knew that I wanted
nothing more than to be welcomed and loved by his family. As I filled
with confusion, shame, and fear, my apologies started pouring out. But
my apologies fell short.

I sat as he stood and continued to express his righteous anger. I was
showing my sinful side and it was his job as a fellow believer to point
it out. He'd point it out over and over until he believed I had learned.

In the end, I can remember feeling horrible yet thankful that he didn't
discard me. (*Yesss, I was thankful to him.* After all, he was favoring me
with his presence and his good opinion.)

My commitment had only served to enforce my need to apologize, *to
make it okay.* Codependency at its finest.

A secret foundation was being laid within me.

I say secret because nobody knew it was there—including me. And that
foundation was replacing my own. Basically, I had left my own foundation open for discussion. But I guess you could say I decided not to
participate in the discussion.

What the Actual Crap Happened to You?

I used to be the girl who graduated from college at the top of her class, full of hope, ready to do something important. I had expectations for myself. I was going to travel. I was going to have a career, get married, then have a baby a few years later.

I had plans to speak and lead other women who were struggling. God made it clear to me that he was going to use my experience and pain to relate to other women. That was a gift I kept stored in my heart. I was completely confident of this.

I could see it. It was clear to me.

Did you ever have plans? Did you have a picture in your mind of your future? Think about the last time you had a vision that didn't revolve around another person.

Yes. It is okay to have dreams with other people. Absolutely. If the dreams in your heart are not replaced with something better, something that lights you up, then are you part of those dreams? Or are you compromising and helping another person reach *their* dreams?

We dated for over a year before breaking up. I can't remember why. I can only remember being confused. I believed I was supposed to marry this man … and he didn't feel the same.

I prayed every day for guidance. I was desperate for him to come back to me. And he did.

Getting back together after that breakup added more knots to that tether from me to him.

I had begun to dress in ways that I knew he would like. I wore colors he liked and fixed my hair the way I knew he liked it. I did whatever I could to get his attention.

He made sure to let me know if I was showing too much skin, if my pants were too tight, or if my shirt was too low. And even though part of me was annoyed and felt shame when he told me, he always explained to me that he was telling me things I had just never been taught.

You see, he loves to teach. And he can find moments to teach and explain things from his perspective. He was not only passionate about teaching, but he was also compelled to share his wisdom regularly.

A good gaslighting narcissist can spot every gap in your foundation. They will make you feel as if they are redeeming those spaces with their love and guidance. And every place where their words take up residence will soon require mental renovation.

Guess who does a mental renovation without telling you their plans for reconstruction? The same person you gave yourself to.

You're in it deep now. It's beginning to feel more natural to think like him. And you're kind of okay with that.

The groundwork of gaslighting has been laid and now mental frameworks are beginning to take shape inside of *your* mind. And he didn't even have to ask you if he could begin this work in your mind. You opened the door and he talked his way into every space in your head.

DECISION MAKING

With all of his wisdom and teaching being passed on to me regularly, it was becoming more apparent that I needed his opinion to make decisions. After all, if I had hoped to marry this guy, then I wanted to consult him on everything. That's how it's supposed to be.

I had been soaking up all the lessons taught by other women for years. They spoke frequently of dying to self and being a helpmate. It sounded so amazing, so lifegiving.

In Bible studies, we hear it. In rooms surrounded by other girls, we learn it. We are to be gentle, humble, and have quiet spirits. We are to love sacrificially. We are to support men. We are to help them. We are to complete each other.

Women are to be submissive and respectful. We are to lead men to Christ by our example. We are to become one flesh, one in body and mind.

I thought that is exactly what I was doing. I was convinced that this man was destined to be my husband. So I was just practicing my role. I was learning what it meant to be a helpmate and be under his headship.

So, when we broke up a second time, I was confused and devastated. Again, he would tell me about her. The girl who he had loved ...

I started it.

He told me that she called him out of the blue after not speaking for years. *What?! What did she want?*

… And he had seen her when he was visiting his old stomping grounds.

No. Nooo. This cannot be happening. I already feel like I am battling a ghost. But she wasn't a ghost. She was very real. Now she was interrupting my dream.

To say the least, I was feeling insecure and unsettled. I was losing sleep. *Was this a joke, God? You told me I am supposed to wait for this man, that he was supposed to be my husband.*

I wanted more from the relationship. My understanding of his feelings was unclear. Clarity was needed. So a few days later, in the middle of dinner, I asked.

"Where am I in comparison to her?"

"My feelings for her were here," he said as he motioned with his hand, "and my feelings for you are about here," he finished while lowering his hand several inches.

I choked out, "Well, I guess there's not much left to say. I don't want to keep coming in second place after all this time." It was all I could muster through my tears. I stopped eating and got up to leave the room.

I wanted him to choose and be done with it.

This girl who had lied to him over and over and over … he had stronger feelings for her than for me. He blamed her for his mistrust, and yet he cared more about her. It made no sense to me. A stronger person might have been done with the relationship right there. A person who understood her worth might've had a clearer view.

That was it. Two years into a relationship that I truly believed was headed to marriage and it was over. I told him I didn't want to see him again.

Well, that was a big, fat lie.

I didn't know how I could even breathe without him. So, when my roommate got engaged the next week, let's just say I wasn't exactly happy for her. She hadn't even put six months into her relationship and she was getting married in a few months.

What the heck?

But I did it. I cut him off.

Until I saw him at an event.

Things were not going so well for me. My parents were getting a divorce. My stepdad was divorcing my mom and I was very close to him. I wanted to go see him in person. I wanted to drive a few hours to talk to him.

I rationalized that this was something I shouldn't do alone. I might be too upset to drive myself. So, naturally, I needed someone who knew the relationship to go with me. So, when I saw him at that event, it had to be fate.

I asked him if he would go.

What the hell was I thinking? What was wrong with me?

He was so kind and seemingly compassionate. He seemed to feel really bad for me. I remember the two chairs we sat in. I remember what I was wearing. I remember the look on his face as he listened.

Clearly, he pitied me.

I put myself in a position to receive pity. And somehow he managed to make me feel like I was overreacting while simultaneously confirming that he was the only person who could be trusted to go with me.

I told myself it had nothing to do with wanting him back and everything to do with him being my closest friend. I'd begun telling myself a lot of things.

No trip was planned. I dropped the idea. Not sure how I managed to let that one go, but I did.

Four weeks later, it was volleyball season. We had always been on a co-ed team together. I called the coach and told him that I'd be sitting out this season because I didn't want to be around my ex. He tried to talk me out of it, but I just knew I couldn't handle seeing him a couple of times every week.

Two days later, he shows up at my door bearing gifts. I was completely confused and had no idea what to think.

He had talked to the coach. When he realized that he would not get to see me each week, he didn't like that. So, he naturally went out and bought me the latest knee pads that would protect my knees.

Smiles … so many flirty smiles were covering his face. He knew how to melt me. I don't think I lasted two minutes before my guard was down.

When he asked me to go visit his family the next month, I basically moved heaven and earth, risking my job to leave town in a week.

On that trip, he proposed and finally told me he loved me. I sobbed like a baby.

Finally, all of my dreams were being realized …

Was he my only dream?

During the engagement, it became more and more apparent that I needed to trust him. He was going to be my husband and wives were supposed to submit and trust in their husbands.

So, he decided how much we would spend. He decided how much I could budget for my food each week. He decided what financial plan we would follow. He decided what church would be best. He decided when we would say "I love you" to each other.

Now, I might have spoken with him about these things, but I was following his lead. He always talked me over to his way of thinking. Even though I didn't understand why we couldn't say "I love you" all the time, he reminded me how uncomfortable it was for him to hear it and to say it.

It hurt, but I followed. I stopped saying it.

Again. That should've been a clue … but I trusted him. He was my world. I thought he was supposed to be my world. We were becoming one flesh, right?

I could not see that I was slowly disappearing as I took on *his* flesh.

We got married and he decided when we would have sex. He knew what was best. He had a plan.

It made me feel like a weak, desperate person for wanting him. I thought all couples had tons of sex on their honeymoons. My friends all told me that is what they did.

He told me they were exaggerating. That it wasn't realistic. After all, he was a real man, a mature man.

We fought on our honeymoon. He told me it was normal. Of course it was normal. We were both tired and had just undergone intense stress getting ready for the wedding.

Right. Of course he was right. And he loved me. I had to believe him. I had to.

Walk the Line

I now carried that shovel around with me. Every day, I would dig a little deeper and put that shovel into my purse like it was the keys to my car. Without thinking, I just did it.

The place of my burial was always with me. It was an open grave. I was digging it and he was saving the dirt.

We'd only been married a few weeks when I was about to cross a line I could not see …

Our first official church visit as a married couple was checked off the list. Afterwards, I was waiting in the car while he grabbed a few things from his old roommate. When he bent down in front of the car, I tapped the horn.

That was it. A horn tap. I had no idea what I had just done.

I thought I was being silly and having fun. He didn't agree. At all. I was wholly stunned by his reaction to my joke.

What began as a joke turned into a lecture. A raging lecture of how rude and inconsiderate I was.

I sat there in my lavender church dress and matching sandals while tears relentlessly poured over my face. My mind was racing as I tried to defend myself. Words from women at church were flooding my head.

"Pull over!! Let me out! I want out!" came screaming out of my lips about ten miles from our new apartment.

His truck came to an abrupt halt.

I continued, "You are not loving me like Christ loves the church!" Righteous indignation and my crushed heart forced the words out of my mouth. "Jesus would be ashamed of you! He would never—"

My body was half-in-half-out of the truck as he cut my words in half by flipping me off and pulling away, screeching his tires.

It was June in the south. It was hot. It was the middle of the day. And I was walking down the side of the road in a dress and sandals carrying my Bible, cheeks wet with hot tears.

A man and his son saw me and offered me a ride. Needless to say, his opinion of a man who would drop his wife off on the side of the road was pretty low.

Three hours later, my adoring husband walked in the door of our love nest. He found me hiding in our bed unsure of what to do with myself. And he was pissed.

"Pshh. Yeah. That's what I thought. What a bitch."

It was the first time he called me a name. He chose a label that he knew was a major trigger for me. He chose to use the one word that had caused me more hurt than any other word from my childhood. And he delivered it with seething venom.

That day, he knelt in front of me and vowed to never call me a bitch again. I believed him. I always believed him.

It was a vow he would break over and over.

It was years before I would share that story. Nineteen years to be exact.

I couldn't tell anyone he had called me a bitch. I couldn't tell anybody because it might hurt him. They might think negative things about him. He was my husband. My *choice*. To tell anybody about what happened would be an act of betrayal.

Plus, he said he was sorry. He apologized.

Not to mention, people might misunderstand our marriage. They might judge it. So, I didn't tell my friends, and I especially didn't tell my family.

Afterall, I had made a vow eleven years prior to that day. I *would* have a Godly marriage. That meant putting him first. I was no longer my own.

Our marriage had not reached the one month mark and I had learned to protect him, make excuses for him, and refrain from giving out any information that might be seen as ugly.

The fear was there … but I was holding it at bay. I was shoving it way, waaaaay down. Let's just say the place I shoved it to was the midnight zone of my soul. It's hard for anything living to thrive in the midnight zone. People can't really survive there.

I was oblivious to what was happening. That's the thing about gaslighting. You don't usually know it's happening to you. If you knew, you probably wouldn't fall prey to it.

Gaslighting gets its name from an old British stage play called *Gas Light*. The husband basically manipulates his wife into believing she is losing her mind. Gaslighting is actually a narcissistic way to abuse people while meeting the abuser's need to feel okay about themselves.

The abuser makes the victim question her memory. Essentially, the narcissist turns her into his emotional and logic-distorted slave. He does this naturally. It is second-nature to him.

Gaslighters are not emotionally and mentally firing on all cylinders, but they have no idea this is the case. It is even likely that they don't know they're gaslighting you.

And yet, they are definitely gaslighting you. The habit is pervasive.

Here's the thing. People who gaslight others have very strong narcissistic tendencies. Wanna take a guess what some typical characteristics of narcissists might be?

Narcissists are charming. Yesss. They know how to work people to the point of admiration.

Narcissists know how to read people. My therapist told me that narcissists are experts at reading people.

Combine charm with the ability to read people. This means they know how to pick people out who are vulnerable to their charm and use it to their advantage.

Notice I said "vulnerable." You won't know it's happening. He picked you on purpose. You're looking for connection. *You're trusting.*

Please don't hear me say you're dumb. You're not. Narcissists have a knack for picking strong people.

Narcissists are masters at making you feel connected. It's all part of their process for meeting their needs … and wooing you into the gaslighting trance.

> *"How many narcissists does it take to screw in a lightbulb?*
> *None. They don't use lightbulbs, they use gaslighting!"*
>
> —Anonymous

Ain't that the truth.

ARGUING

It has been said that engaging in an argument with a narcissist is a whole lot like being placed under arrest. You know your Miranda Rights? Yep. It's like that. Anything you say can and will be used against you.

Nobody can back you into a corner better than a gaslighting narcissist.

When our marriage first started, I thought we could have discussions. I thought I could disagree with him and he would hear me.

In a mutually respectful marriage, people have discussions. They might be heated. They are probably uncomfortable at some point. But they both have a voice, and they each walk away feeling heard.

I know. Sounds like a unicorn marriage in Utopia.

But, I promise you, those marriages are real. I have seen them. I am friends with those people. Don't misunderstand me. They are not perfect. As a matter of fact, they are both completely imperfect.

The difference? These couples *see* each other. They see all of the bad and the good. Fully embracing the other person allows both spouses to be free to express themselves and to authentically love one another.

For these couples, it's not just about being committed to their marriage. It is also about being fully committed to empowering their partners to be the best versions of themselves. To know and be known. There is authentic, undeniable beauty in that.

When we had discussions, I entered them with a little fear because I hate conflict. So, speaking up took courage for me. I knew I was smart and had a knack for communicating. I would be able to state my side and be the helpmate God had created me to be.

Our discussions usually began with him expressing his concerns over something he had noticed, something that was bothering him. And I almost always found myself on the defensive. I was just trying to defend myself.

Somehow, my behavior had offended him or been inconsiderate. It was his job, *his duty*, as my husband to tell me what I had done wrong. He was helping me. He was simply pointing me to Christ and helping me be a better wife.

It was becoming very obvious throughout any discussion that I needed to apologize for my behavior. I had no idea how I had been so wrong without purposely doing anything to him.

However, he had thoroughly thought through his side of the discussion. He laid out his case and there was no room for any disagreement. At least, not the way that I disagreed.

I didn't disagree *the right way*.

If I was disagreeing the right way, then he would have been able to listen to me.

But, of course, I wasn't. I never disagreed properly.

So that's why he was upset with my thoughts. I was a poor communicator.

Again, it was my fault. I needed to apologize.

I had screwed up. He was right. I was wrong. *How could I have been so insensitive? I was so horribly insensitive that I didn't even realize I was being inconsiderate!!*

Thankfully, he was so wise that he could see my mistakes even when I didn't know I was making them. (Insert my best sarcastic tone here.)

He had skillfully talked me into a corner and then verbally pushed me into a kneeling position. What else is a person to do other than humble themselves before their wiser counterpart?

I walked into those first "discussions" thinking we were on the same level.

We were not on the same level. He always made sure to correct my posture, *to humble me.* And expected me to be grateful for it.

He told me an appropriate response would be to say thank you to him for his input.

No. I am not kidding.

It didn't feel right … Something felt wrong, but I knew I had come from a background of parents with broken marriages. And, I kept that shovel handy. So I'd just bury those unhelpful thoughts.

Gaslighting causes you to question yourself, to question your responses to situations, and to question your own thoughts and feelings.

When you are being gaslighted by someone you love, by someone you *want* to love, nothing in you wants to believe something awful is happening to you. And the narcissism present in the object of your affection will keep you from believing it.

You are in a full-on deception game. But you don't know you're in a game. So, you don't have instructions. You don't know how to play. And the rules keep changing.

The rules change according to his purposes and moods. The game is still new at this point, so you can't predict any of those moods.

You're in a game of real-life Mau.

Have you played Mau? It's a card game. It's not like rummy or war. This card game has no instructions. Like zip. Families love to play this card game and bring in outsiders to join.

I say outsiders because the family already has a clue what's going on. And if you have joined in the game, nobody tells you what they already know. So, you are sitting there, trying to figure out what the heck is going on.

In Mau, the rules seem to change as the game goes along. New rules pop up. And hopefully you guess some of the rules along the way so you can keep playing.

But never. Not once. Will you be given the rules ahead of time.

Like I said, real-life Mau.

I know that's what I found myself in. I couldn't keep up with his moods or his rules or my rules. My rules were different from his. And I didn't get to make any of them—at least, not unless they were approved.

My Rules

My rules. Wow ... there have been so many ...

Be helpful at all times, but not in a way that makes him feel anything he perceives negatively.

Be truthful, but not about anything he cannot admit or that he has a different perspective on.

Be loving, but don't say it out loud because it makes him uncomfortable.

Be affectionate, but only when he wants it.

Be supportive—even when I completely disagree and know he is in the wrong.

Be respectful—even if he is being condescending and oppressive.

Be attentive—even when my child is crying, I must not shift my eyes.

Be thin, but don't spend too much time working out because that averts my focus from the home.

Be pleasant, but not when I am defending him to others.

Be apologetic—even when I've done nothing wrong because *he feels* that I've wronged him.

Be social, but not when he doesn't feel like it.

Be friendly, but not to people who rub him the wrong way.

Be a disciplinarian, but not when he can do it better.

Be available—even if I am doing my own work.

Be organized, but not in a way that he doesn't understand.

Be attractive, but do not draw attention to myself.

Be sexual—even if he has been mean to me all week, I must accept his advances.

Be tidy—even with several young kids, I must keep them organized.

Be frugal, but do not store hand-me-downs for the children or ask him to use generic products that are on sale.

Be clean—no matter how my schedule changes with several children, keep the house clean.

Be communicative, but not in a way that he misinterprets.

Be understanding—even when he is completely illogical.

Be funny, but not in a way he deems socially inappropriate.

Now, those are just the standard ones that I had to remember every single day. There were random rules that came up situationally.

If I could just remember all of the rules most of the time, then our weeks would go semi-smoothly. No rage fests. For me, that was a win.

I might have felt more and more like I was a horrible person in need of help, but at least I wasn't screamed at and no walls were punched. That was another win for me.

I had begun to learn it was my fault. Failing to stick to his rules was an obvious sign of my need to change and mature. *He* had begun to meticulously explain to me that *he* was wise and mature, but *I* was definitely not.

Gaslighting leaves no bruises, no broken bones. It crushes your mind and your spirit.

You are the frog. The frog in a pot of water. It's water, so you are in there just a swimmin'. Sure, you're confined, but it's water. You love water. Water is like home.

When the water starts to warm up, you barely notice. It feels different, wrong perhaps. However, you don't do anything because you're adapting.

That's gaslighting for you. It's a gradual process that lulls you into adaptability. And you know what adaptability means?

Survival.

SURVIVAL MODE

Adaptability has its place.

Think about reality TV. No, not like *Naked and Afraid*. Eww. More like *Survivor*.

The main goal is to be the last survivor and win the big money. The people on *Survivor* end up being on a team. While on that team, they form alliances.

You cannot form an alliance if nobody likes you or if you're seen as lazy. To stay in the game, you have to work really hard physically and mentally.

You have to push yourself physically and mentally while dealing with people who either constantly feel threatened by your presence or want to threaten your presence.

The game of *Survivor* is insane. The contestants eat crazy, disgusting food, they participate in demanding physical challenges, and their food sources are pretty limited.

Meanwhile, you have to balance being likable with being competitive and wicked smart. You cannot relax and shut off your brain. Ever.

To survive, you must adapt. Every new situation must be met with your adaptability if you want to make it through to the next challenge.

Survive or be gone. Period.

People talk about you behind your back. They plan and scheme. *You* talk about other people. *You* plan and scheme.

Players do things and say things they never thought they would do. *Whatever it takes to survive.*

In *Survivor*, you must adapt every single day. It quite literally keeps all of the players in survival mode.

Survival mode is exhausting.

If you are in an intimate relationship with a gaslighting narcissist, you may be living in survival mode. Ask yourself:

- Do I feel helpless and alone?
- Have I been sleeping well?
- Am I constantly rushing to get things done, but never get caught up?
- Have I become disconnected from friends and family?
- Am I doing well just to make it through each day?
- How often do I laugh and enjoy my day?
- Am I constantly on the verge of snapping?
- Do I think I'm the only one who can handle things the right way?
- Do I find myself reacting rather than responding to situations?

Chances are you can relate to a lot of these questions. You probably don't like your answers. I know that my answers feel gross to me. I have been at a place where I could answer yes to several of them.

You have begun to live in fight, flight, freeze, or fawn mode. It's chronic. Your body stays at attention, ready for the next problem to come up that you must deal with.

You learn survival behaviors. Very unhealthy survival behaviors. You might not have noticed the anxiety that snuck in and took root in your body.

At this point in the game—and make no mistake, it is a game—your heart is all in. This partnership reels you in and pushes you away over and over and over.

What we don't realize is that the body is cooperating with the mind. Stressors are happening around us. They are happening *to* us. And our bodies respond accordingly.

Hormones are released. That's what happens in stressful situations. A little alert goes off in the hypothalamus and it immediately goes into action by telling the body to release those lovely stress hormones.

Stress hormones are supposed to be helpful. Their job is to help us respond to stressful situations by reacting quickly. For most of us, we are not trained to deal with those danger signals on a daily basis.

You don't wake up one day and think, *You know. It would be a great idea to prepare myself to deal with verbal abuse from my spouse. I think I'll do some mental training exercises for that.*

No. People who expect to go into combat, be interrogated, be threatened and tortured—those are the people who mentally train to prepare their minds and bodies to handle stress.

Marriage isn't supposed to be like that. It's not designed for it. You're supposed to feel safe walking into that relationship with an open heart and bearing your soul. You're supposed to be completely vulnerable and in turn feel loved and accepted.

That's where it gets tricky.

You probably did walk into it feeling just like that. Oh my word ... what a fabulous feeling. You believe you are loved exactly how you should be. It feels beautiful, right? It's as if you can inhale happiness when you're together.

You feel so safe.

He *knows* you feel safe. He knows that *he* did that for you. (Insert applause and pats on the back for him here because he has rescued you.)

So, when he starts pointing out your less-desirable qualities, you believe him when he tells you it's his role as your husband. You believe him when he says he is supposed to point out your sin because you can't do it on your own.

Lordy lordy ... I can remember a single friend asking me what "marriage was like so far." I'm embarrassed to tell you what I said. Oh my word ...

With tearful passion, I responded to my friend. "Marriage is like having someone hold up a mirror to your sin. It's having another person so close to you that they tell you things you need to change."

I went on to explain how amazing it was to be cared for like that. Yeah. Yeah, I did.

Eww. That. Is. Gross.

But, dang. I believed it. I had to believe it. He was the spiritual leader in our home. He would never lie. He loved me. And I just didn't know any better. He told me I just couldn't see what I was doing wrong.

What a hero.

It's like this ...

The groundwork has been laid. And the hooks are firmly attached to your soul.

You're completely taken off-guard when this same, helpful man who regularly offers up his suggestions to you is pissed that you ask him to take out the trash. The trash he agreed to take out.

You are not seen as being helpful. You are seen as mothering him. Your polite request to ask him to do something he promised to do is met with utter disdain and contempt.

How dare you.

How dare you assume that he needs you to tell him to do something. No. That isn't going to work for him. You have no right. He is a grown man. (Nevermind that the trash is overflowing.)

This turns into an argument. It's in this argument where he really begins to assert his authority. He takes your little eyeballs and pries them open to see the truth that you are just not capable of understanding.

He would never argue unless he believed he was right. So, in arguing about the trash, he absolutely knew he was right and you were wrong.

Confused by this, you question him. He tells you that he believes he will be right at least eighty, if not ninety, percent of the time when you argue with him.

Well, now that we've gotten that little fact out of the way in the first couple of months of marriage, everything will just go swimmingly.

That doesn't feel right, but you bury it.

I buried it. I mean … Why not? We all know that I kept a shovel handy for burying myself.

So, when the next argument happens, I remember what he said. I'm nervous. I'm really nervous.

The mouth that has communicated to groups of people many times? It's completely dry. Those hands that have dribbled a ball in front of a crowd, held a microphone in front of hundreds of people? They're sweating.

Yep. Those fight or flight hormones are kicking in. Lucky me. I'm surviving. Nothing quite like sweating your way through an argument.

Guess what? Tense muscles, fertility problems, lack of sexual desire, rapid heart, sweaty palms, heartburn, fast breathing, immune system struggling, can't sleep … All of that can happen to your body when you live in survival mode.

Survival mode serves a great purpose. But it's supposed to be for a temporary purpose. We are not supposed to live there. Our bodies don't like it.

We can function in survival mode. We can walk through our daily activities. We can go to church. We can sing lullabies to our kids. We can survive.

There is this pride about being labeled a survivor. But being a survivor and living in survival mode are not the same thing. Nothing feels heroic about living in survival mode.

Survival mode is another way to say you're living with toxic stress. Toxic stress affects you mentally and physically. As your mind scrambles to be safe, your body feels it.

Maybe you lose weight, maybe you can't lose weight, maybe your hair falls out, your jaw is tight all the time, or you have a constant backache. I have lost my hair four times (not including hair loss after having babies). It was years before I realized that I clench my jaw when I'm stressed.

Survival mode is no way to truly live.

Meeting You Where You Are

Survival mode is exhausting. It's soul crushing. It takes over without permission. And my body is used to it. It can slip right into survival mode because it's been there so many times.

And yet, here I am. Writing a book from an emotionally healthy state of mind. I couldn't do what I'm doing if I were living my life in survival mode.

As you have gathered by now, I am not a sugar-coating kind of person. I know the road I've walked has just plain sucked. There are no fancy words for it. Sometimes life just feels like a sucktastrophy. (You're welcome to borrow that word. I made it up just for this.)

You may be living in the middle of your sucktastrophy. It probably feels like it will never end. You're looking down the longest, darkest tunnel of life and you are still waiting for that light to come.

I can remember feeling like my tunnel would go on until I died or he died. And the loss of hope was nearly unbearable. I didn't want to kill myself, but I didn't know how to live either. Does that make sense?

Survival mode is not living. It's existing. You and I are meant for more than existing. I know that I know that I *knowww* my life has purpose. And my purpose isn't validated by a man or by my children.

Am I a mom for a purpose? Yes. Absolutely. Is it my only purpose? Nope.

Was I married for a purpose? Yes. Absolutely. Do I know every reason that I was married to someone who caused me so much trauma? Heck no.

I want you to know that I am still *pro* marriage. Marriage is not meant to put you into a constant state of survival mode. It's meant for you to thrive, to make you more than you are without that person. (That isn't to say you aren't enough by yourself. *You are.*)

Marriage is multiplication. It's not addition. It's definitely not subtraction. There isn't another relationship on earth that can multiply you the way an amazing marriage can. I've seen it.

God has brought multiple couples into my life who've been married over twenty years, and they are best friends. They're not perfect, but they are incredible partners. They respect each other. They love each other. And they are *for* each other.

They are not surviving. They are thriving.

I'm single. I'm healing. And I am whole all by myself.

I have reached the place where I know that I am a gift. I am a blessing to whatever man is lucky enough to be in a relationship with me. Rushing into a relationship to fill loneliness, soothe fear, or avoid facing the work of healing isn't going to happen.

I am worth the work it takes to love myself. I am worth the wait.

And so are you.

CONFUSION

Cyndi Lauper got it right when she sang, "Caught up in circles, confusion is nothing new."

Relationships are very confusing when you've been made to feel like you're wrong, you've messed up repeatedly, you've disappointed them, and you need to make changes ... But, then.

Then, they bring in positive reinforcement.

Damn that positive reinforcement.

You are such a good cook. You could open your own restaurant.

The house looks great. You could decorate for a living.

You look really pretty. I like that outfit.

I'm proud of you. What a great job.

These compliments often serve your gaslighter.

Let's think about that. Does the thing he noticed benefit him in some way? Can he use it to brag about you to others, does it make him feel good, or does it make him look good to others?

Three hours ago, he let you know that the tone you used when speaking to him was disrespectful. He made sure you understood how wrong you were by repeating himself over and over.

Hammering it into your mind over and over is his special gift to you. He will not let up until he believes you get the message. It doesn't matter if you have already acknowledged him. It doesn't matter if you've apologized.

He isn't finished.

And he will not stop delivering his message until he is finished.

Your words are wasted on him. He can't hear them. He doesn't want to hear them. *He is doing his job.* You should just shut up and be thankful that he cares so much.

Later, he'll tell you that you never apologized. He will tell you that you are making that up. You must've just thought you said it. So, you question yourself.

And you apologize. Again.

Keep in mind, it must be done when he is ready to hear it. The words must be right, your countenance must be humble, and your tone should sound genuine.

He feels so much better.

You may feel like crap. But he doesn't. He got everything off of his chest and at the same time helped you see what you did wrong.

Now he's ready for sex.

Your connection feels broken. You want to reconnect with him, so of course, you want to be intimate. You want to give yourself to him and feel connected again.

The cycle is complete. Your confusion caused you to feel insecure, but his desire for you gave you a sense of security.

Contempt.
Confusion.
Contrition.
Connection.

Your role is becoming clearer to you. He is showing you who you need to be within your relationship.

Your gaslighter knows that safety and security are important to women. He knows that feeling normal and stable in your own home is something that you crave.

This cycle of showing you contempt for whatever you've done to wound him, your confusion about the event, your expected contrition, and your desired connection—it leaves you feeling off-kilter and unstable.

Lucky for you, he will now position himself as the person to make you feel normal and stable.

Yeah … lucky, lucky me. That story was a long thread woven throughout my marriage. It was that same thread that left me feeling like I had prostituted myself.

People say that relationships are all about give and take. Well, the gaslighter is perfectly in charge of this. He will take away your stability and give it back to you by making himself the hero of your ever-changing story.

You *will* keep looking to him. You can't help it. You want him to make you feel stable. You believe that it is healthy and right and good to feel stability from a strong partner.

You adapt to this confusion.

You are becoming more and more adept in your ability to adapt to different states of confusion.

That little feeling in the pit of your stomach? The one you hate. The uncomfortable, knot-forming feeling? You dig around in your coping toolbox for something to make it go away. That's what you do.

Think.

Think hard and remember when you first noticed something was just *off*.

Remember the first time you mentally questioned yourself and chose his explanation over your own.

The first time he dismissed you, and you dismissed yourself.

Honestly? I had some pretty clear signals while we were dating. If I had known myself, known what gaslighting looked like, maybe I'd have caught it early.

But, I didn't. You didn't either, or you probably wouldn't be reading this.

The life I was living was no longer my own. I had begun living for him, for his pleasure. And my pleasure? My pleasure was slowly escaping me.

Hindsight

When he got angry over little things his roommates did, I believed his rationalizations. I bought into his logic.

When he told me where I should live, I bragged to my friends about how much he cared and started making plans to move.

Everything he did—*all of it*—had a reason. He explained everything to me.

And when I didn't understand, when I couldn't make sense of it, he taught me that it was because something was wrong with my thinking. Normal people would understand his point of view.

That.

That is what he did to my brain. He convinced me that my failure to understand and believe any of his reasons, my failure to comprehend his rationale, *my confusion* wasn't normal.

He was normal. *His* thoughts were normal. *His* reasons were normal. *His* actions were normal. *He* was like everybody else.

It was me. I was the one who wasn't thinking about things the right way. I was the one who had muddled thinking.

I needed his thoughts to help me have my own. I had begun to trust his thoughts more than my own.

And he was there to help. He made it his goal to be helpful. He made it his goal to teach me.

Lucky me.

Lucky, *lucky* me. I had partnered with someone who was ready, willing, and able to teach me for the rest of my life ... teach me how to think, how to love, how to have relationships, how to worship God.

He made sure to let me know what a catch I had in him.

Yes. Lucky me.

And you know what? I felt lucky.

AMMUNITION

You never quite know what will add fuel to the fire. Unlike your toolbox that is fairly empty, his toolbox is growing and changing on the daily.

While he is training you to trust him and give yourself to him, he is taking all of it in and packing it neatly into his little toolbox to use when he sees fit.

You tell him all about yourself. You tell him about your struggles. You tell him about your childhood. Everything that broke your heart and crushed your spirit, you confide in him with all of it.

It feels good. He listens so attentively. He asks questions. And he remembers.

You'd better believe he remembers.

There are so many stories from childhood that you share. Like the first time your mom slapped you across the face and called you a bitch. You recall how horrible it was and how much it wounded you to be called that name during an argument about your dad.

The times you did not validate your mother's relationship, she would call you a bitch. It was not often, but the times she did use that word were very pointed.

It is those incidents that marked you and made the word "bitch" a trigger for you. The memories are painful.

So later when he calls you a bitch, he knows exactly what he's doing. He knows exactly how deeply he is striking a nerve. Your heartstrings have been exposed and he is plucking them *to death*.

Actually, he will use not only your words but he will also hold onto the words used by others to speak about you.

Let's say your mother tells you to stop pouting or whining about something in front of him. Yesss. That's a great one to keep in his back pocket and pull out whenever he feels like it.

How does that one work? Well, I've got news for you. The word "pout" is quite versatile in the hands of a creative person.

For example, when you are discussing the future and know that realistically you won't be able to afford vacation, your natural response is to figure out a way you can make it happen. You're actually getting kind of excited about it.

The two of you come up with a plan to make it happen. The discussion doesn't go very well because you feel dismissed. You don't really understand because you have enough money to do it. You're pretty bummed.

He reluctantly agrees to a plan. You have the money budgeted to do it. You have more than enough money to make it happen. It's not a stretch. It's not even a sacrifice.

But pretty soon, he lets you know that you talked him into it. You basically forced him to do it because you were pouting. He tells you that your mom was right, you do pout.

Mmmhmm. Good times.

Two labels were put on me within the first months of marriage: bitch and pouter.

He managed to use two hurtful things from my past within three little months. In three little months, we sure were becoming one ... I was becoming *less me* and *more him*.

Bitch and pouter. Two words that were attached to pain and hurt. Two words he knew would make me *feel* it. He wanted me to feel how much I had wronged him.

You see, it is of utmost importance that you feel it deeply when a gas-lighter makes their move. When a gaslighting narcissist calls you a name, you can bet it will hurt. They don't pick a random word.

They've listened to you carefully and stored things away for their pur-poses. An arsenal of pain is at their disposal. Each tool serves a purpose. Every one of those tools is meant to be used in the right place at the right time to inflict as much pain as possible.

And when they've finished using their tools, while you are feeling the rawness of your wounds, you will also come to realize that you caused your own wound.

That's right.

A gaslighter will wound you and convince you that you caused your own wound. They will do it so well that you won't even realize what is happening.

It's as if they slipped a little piece of shit into your Cocoa Puffs. It's brown. It blends right in. You know it tastes a little funny ... but most of the bites taste normal.

So you just swallow it down and keep eating it until the bad taste in your mouth goes away. You barely notice the aftertaste.

No worries. I'm sure he has guilt-flavored gum to cover up the taste of the shit he just fed you.

Ammunition comes in whatever form he chooses. It's strategic. And in the beginning it is wildly unpredictable.

In the first year of marriage, I couldn't predict it and I definitely wasn't expecting it. So, I walked around hopeful and vulnerable.

Why?

Well, because marriage is a partnership. It's built on trust. You are meant to be open and vulnerable, to believe the best, to give them your heart, and to take the good with the bad.

That fifteen-year-old girl was alive and well inside of me. Eyes on the prize. She was going to be the one who set the example of a Christ-centered marriage for the rest of her family. She was skipping around in there, ignoring the pain and acrid taste of someone else's crap.

Sometimes ammunition comes in the form of supported logic.

There's a First Time for Everything

The first time he punched a hole in something, we'd only been married about six months. We were living in a one-bedroom apartment. As you can imagine, there was nowhere to hide, nowhere to have personal space.

I can't tell you what made him mad that day. I can only tell you that he was pissed about something and holding me responsible for it.

Naturally, I followed him around our tiny space trying to make peace. Instead of working it out, he only became more enraged and put his fist through our bathroom door as a result.

A few months later when he bloodied his knuckles on a support beam, I was scared. In my mind, he was violent. I was completely freaked out.

I was crying and talking and telling him over and over that it wasn't okay. He was completely unmoved.

No … That's not true.

He thought my reaction was pretty funny and most certainly way too dramatic. Yes. I was overreacting. I had to be because he told me I was.

To prove to me that his behavior was fine, he put me on the phone with his buddy. His buddy had been married longer than us. I trusted him.

When he assured me that punching things was a normal behavior for guys, I argued at first. But he made light of it and just kept telling me it was nothing to worry about, not a big deal.

He found someone to support his logic.

And he used that logic to defeat me.

He wasn't hateful about it. Nope. He was thoughtful. He came up with a plan to prove my silly overreaction wrong. He used someone I trusted to do it.

When two people sneak shit into your Cocoa Puffs, you swallow it, you tell yourself that you taste nothing bad, and you begin to lose faith in your own senses.

THE BUDDY SYSTEM

Many adults who went on field trips in public school or have kiddos in public school are familiar with the buddy system.

It was a big deal to partner up before stepping one foot on that bus. Once you were sitting in your seat, whoever sat next to you was going to be your buddy. For the entire field trip.

Wherever you go, your buddy goes. Wherever you sit, your buddy sits beside you. Whenever you head to the restroom, your buddy does too.

It was the buddy system at its best.

Remember that lovely boy doll with the brown hair and primary-colored clothes? No? Well, allow me to refresh your memory with a little song.

"My Buddy, My Buddy, Wherever I go, he goes. My Buddy, My Buddy, I'll teach him everything that I know. My Buddy and me, like to climb up a tree. My buddy and me, We're the best friends that could be!"

A cute, little blonde boy rode around on his Big Wheel while carrying My Buddy on his lap. Yes, that doll went with him everywhere.

You're welcome.

The teacher knew something that her young students did not. Strength and safety came in numbers.

You know what else? Intimidation comes in numbers. The more people who seem to stand against you, the more intimidated you feel, the more you doubt yourself and question your mind.

The buddy system works to the gaslighter's advantage.

One day, you will have done something to disappoint him. He will take it personally. (They always do.) And he will let you know exactly how you've wronged him.

For example, he was frequently convinced that I had been talking about him with my friends. Did he ever have proof? No. He never needed to be there. He didn't need to hear a word.

One night, when he came home at the end of my girls' night, he walked in while everyone was still gathered. Nothing much was said. Just a few casual greetings before all of the girls went back to their homes.

That was it.

Harmless, right?

No. Not a chance that it was harmless. He knows, *he KNOWS*, they were looking at him weird. So, I had clearly been talking crap about him.

Immediately, I go straight into defending myself. I genuinely have no idea what he is talking about. I am completely confused by the accusation. My words are stuck in my throat. My mind is racing.

I continue to fumble through my defense as the hurt strangles my heart and a new feeling begins to familiarize itself with my entire being. Fear. There it is. Creeping in.

He is on a roll now, telling me all about his wisdom and insight. Obviously, I am lying. He sees the truth. He had read the room.

Nothing I say is helping. My words are being twisted as soon as they leave my mouth.

And then he backs up all his accusations by saying this, "My friends were right about you."

Wait. What?! Who?

I ask him what was said and who said it. I want to know. Of course I want to know.

"You have no integrity. Our pastor told me that about you in premarital counseling," he retorts with seething confidence.

The pastor wasn't even in the same room with us, yet he managed to make it seem like they were standing shoulder-to-shoulder, offering support while boring holes into my soul.

He knew he had me. He made sure of it. And he brought invisible reinforcements. The one person who possessed knowledge and discernment.

That's how the buddy system works.

The buddy system will always work *against you* and *for them*. A gaslighter never stops thinking. Their minds are always working to make sure they stay a step ahead.

The buddy system isn't designed to keep you safe. It works to trap you, to corner you. The only way to get out of that corner is to shut up. Your silence will be seen as agreement, submission.

His work here is done.

I was put in my place.

He feels better.

My feelings are irrelevant ... because, frankly, he already knows all of my feelings. There is no need for me to speak.

When things like this happen to me, I just want the horrible feeling in my stomach to go away. I want to feel connected again. So, if silencing my thoughts is what it takes, then that's exactly what I'll do. Whatever it takes to make sure my relationship is okay.

Nevermind that whenever I see my pastor, the one who married us, the one who did our pre-marital counseling, I force a smile to hide my disappointment and hurt.

Nevermind that every time I see my pastor's wife, I wonder if he warned her about my "lack of integrity."

I never consider the possibility that my husband may have been stretching the truth to suit his own needs. That possibility doesn't even cross my mind ...

He hates lies. He prides himself on the truth. He swears up and down, left and right, that *he* is always honest, *he* never lies. Ever.

That's how it works, right?

I believe the best in him.

You believe the best in him.

Believing otherwise just isn't okay. And we *chose* these men. We *chose* to be with them. We *chose* to love them, to commit to them.

And you know what? Now, there is distance between me and my pastor. When he preaches, I feel differently. When I see him, I feel differently. My trust has been broken.

There it is.

More Groundwork

Did you catch what happened? I didn't. I absolutely could not see what was happening.

He was laying the groundwork to be my source of truth. He was making sure that I looked to him first.

And yet … he didn't truly want to be Jesus. He wanted me to love him unconditionally, serve him, and believe his word was truth, but he didn't want me to lean on him too much, or expect too much. And he definitely didn't want to love me and serve me like Jesus.

He wanted all the perks that built him up with none of the hard parts, the sacrificial parts.

Because being married to me *was* his sacrifice. Giving up part of himself *to be married to me* was his sacrifice.

I was blessed to have him. I was blessed to have a direct line to his wisdom and discernment. Yep. Lucky me.

EVERYONE ELSE IS WRONG

My dad used to work at a bank. He learned all about loans and interest and all the different types of accounts. I loved getting the little pieces of free gum and suckers.

When I was older, he worked in an insurance office. He completely dedicated himself to learning as much as possible. He actually got pretty good at selling insurance policies and enjoyed it.

Even though he didn't have a college degree, he attended conferences and became a licensed agent. My dad didn't make a ton of money, but he was dedicated to his craft and managed to provide for us.

After I'd been married for six months, my dad presented me with my insurance policy. It was a life insurance policy that he had been paying on since I was in second grade. He worked really really hard to make those payments no matter how low the bank account had gotten.

My dad wanted to give me a gift. This was the only way he knew how to do it. He was so proud of that insurance policy.

I was shocked. I had no idea that he had a life insurance policy for me. Wow. I knew what a sacrifice my dad had made to make those payments.

"You need to cash that out. It's a crappy policy," my husband said. "You need to get rid of it and just keep the money."

"I can't do that," I protested.

I continued to protest over and over as he grabbed the nails of reason from his pocket and proceeded to hammer them into all of my arguments until he had nailed me against the wall.

My loving husband nailed my mouth shut.

He stated his case over and over to make sure I did what he asked. It didn't matter how I felt about it. It didn't matter how this would make my dad feel.

And it most definitely did not matter what it would do to my relationship with my dad.

My feelings, my relationship—were of no importance.

My point of view did not make sense to him. That automatically meant it wasn't valid. It automatically meant that he must be right.

Month after month, he would ask me if I had canceled that policy yet.

Nothing in me felt okay about canceling that policy. Absolutely nothing. It broke my heart. It made me feel sick. It just felt wrong.

He let me know that I was supposed to leave my parents and cleave to him because that was biblical. I was supposed to trust him above my parents now that we were married. He was my leader and I needed to listen to him. Period.

Otherwise, I wasn't following God.

Yep.

He knew how important it was to me that I follow God in my marriage. He also knew that I was really insecure in my role and scared to death I might get it wrong.

And He wanted me to learn that the people who raised me were wrong and he was right. He wanted me to know that even though my dad had worked in insurance for years, *he knew better*.

He made me tell my dad that I would be canceling the policy that he had paid on for nearly twenty years. And he even told me exactly what I was supposed to tell him.

After all, it was no big deal for me to tell my father that he was just misinformed and that the policy he'd gotten really wasn't worth much and wasn't a good investment for me ... but thank you.

Yes. And I absolutely had to tell him this because the man who I chose to marry, the leader of our home by God-given right, the husband who had been gifted with wisdom and discernment, HE knew that it was the best decision to get rid of that crappy policy.

Within six months of marriage, he drew a line in the sand with a parent who had been nothing but supportive. And he made me shove that line in that parent's face.

My father was crushed. And my siblings who had also been given their own policies were absolutely furious with me. They couldn't believe that I didn't just tell him no.

Everyone else was wrong. My family was wrong.

Only he was right.

He forced me to choose and that choice put up the first wall between my family and me.

He was my husband. I wanted to trust him and put him first. We were *supposed* to put each other first. Right? That is how truly great marriages operated. I wanted a great marriage.

At this point, you might think I was crazy and that you would never ever do that to one of your parents. But the fear of losing my relationship with my husband was real, he had planted those seeds during our dating years. Let's not even get started on the emotional punishment …

Gaslighters Are Always in the Right Place at the Right Time

Gaslighters love to put themselves in the position of being right. They excel at situating themselves in the position of being correct.

That means you are wrong.

Your feelings are wrong. Your feelings are not only wrong, they are trivial. He has managed to take something that put your insides into a tangle of knots and completely trivialize it.

Get used to it. Your feelings will be too big. They will be deemed as ridiculous. You are going to be wrong a lot. There is no room for you to be right. There is only room for him to be right.

And while you're sitting there in all of your wrongness, he will continue to make sure that you understand why you are wrong and how you should really be seeing the situation.

The simple, seemingly innocent fact that you are not naturally seeing situations from his perspective is more confirmation for him that you need help. You need *his* help.

That's right.

It is a good thing he is around to help you see things clearly. To see things correctly.

Lucky you.

Lucky me.

Listen to ... *Your* Gut ?

My brain fought to have my own perspective. My gut tried to alert me. But I was learning that my gut could not be trusted. My gut was wrong.

The little voice inside my mind that alerted me and guided my decisions? The one that tells me when something is not right, or when I need to do something ... It was quickly turning into stifled sounds, hard to distinguish.

I wanted to trust him. I wanted him to have my heart. I wanted to believe he would only ever have my best interest at heart.

Stepping into that, pressing into those thoughts, was making me feel like I was safe. I needed to feel safe. The ache to feel safe was just there, *always*.

Women are hardwired to feel safe and protected. It is how we are made. And that is okay. That is normal and good. There is absolutely nothing wrong with wanting to feel safe with your husband.

He knew it, too. He knew I wanted to feel safe and protected. And he knew I was vulnerable.

Daaaang. That vulnerability would bite me on the arse and come back to haunt me later.

I had so many life lessons to learn, and he was a willing teacher. Always the teacher.

But that was a problem for him. Let me rephrase. I was a problem for him. I had already been through school. I no longer wanted to be a student.

You know those stories about kids who are musical prodigies? It's the story of the young musical genius in search of a teacher ...

Of course, it can't be just any teacher. It is the guy who hasn't taught anybody in twelve years. He is a recluse living on the fourth floor of a high rise surrounded by stacks of newspapers and old books.

But this isn't some random man who teaches piano lessons. This is the man who played Carnegie Hall 253 times with standing ovations. He is a legend.

The mother and son finally track him down and knock on the door. The guy answers gruffly, so they quickly lay out their story. He says no. They beg. He says no again. They beg again, and the mom plays a recording of the little boy playing a piece written by the old musician.

He opens the door and lays out the conditions for him to teach the kid. There is absolutely no doubt that the boy understands he is beyond fortunate to be taught by this piano god.

It's a lot like that.

The gaslighter is teaching you, showing you the right way to think about things. And he wants you to realize how blessed you are to have him watching over you.

He is full of pearls of wisdom and seeds of knowledge, dropping those amazing pearls in front of you, tucking those seeds into your ears.

The spreaders people walk behind to distribute grass seed all over their yards, covering the entire area with its tiny bits of growth potential? Yep. Gaslighters are like living versions of a seed spreader. Contributing their wisdom to the people around them.

Whether they like it or not.

Remember. Gaslighting is second nature to narcissists. You are gradually going to be drawn into a crazymaking cycle.

Meeting You Where You Are

If the words "what the hell??!" have gone through your mind while your face seems to involuntarily contort, don't worry. Mine, too. It took me a solid year to go back and proofread this.

I knew it needed to be done. It practically whispered my name the way you hear in creepy movies. But, I always had other things begging for my attention and a million reasons that those things took precedence over these pages.

And when I finally did force myself to go back through my story, I felt like I'd been in a fight. My head hurt. My body hurt. And I cried, face-in-hands sobbing, as I read through the truth of my life.

Honestly, as I read it, I knew it happened. I knew every word was true. And yet it was like, *How in the hell is this my story?!*

There are several pages of my story that left me feeling completely alone and utterly unprotected. The days when I silently begged for someone to rescue me. The days I curled up on my closet floor hugging myself while his rage rang throughout the house.

Those memories don't disappear. They hang on. They relocate to different spaces in my body ... my hips, my neck, my shoulders, and my chest. The dead center of my chest seems to be their favorite spot to press in and crush.

Your memories don't come gently, do they? They don't tiptoe up or wash over you like a gentle spring rain. No. They pounce. It's like an ongoing game of hide and seek with a group of bullies whose mission in life is to sneak up and scare the living crap out of you.

You're on high alert in an effort to avoid those bullies. And yet, they manage to take you by surprise and before you know it, your heart is racing, your body is tense, and all you can think about is the bully threatening your attempt at peace.

I am learning to be gentle with myself. I don't need more bullies in my life. And that's kind of what we do, right? We beat ourselves up in the struggle. Rather than being our own advocate, we get frustrated and ashamed.

So, this is what I do when the mental and emotional bullies invade my mind. I sit at the table of my soul.

Yep. I picture a dining table. And whatever that part of me is that won't shut up or shut off, I name it. It could be sadness, shame, anxiety, fear, hurt, anger, etc. I literally look at this darn feeling as another part of me.

Sitting at my table is another version of me but it's anger. It's the anger that just reared its ugly head and seemed to take over my whole body. And now she is sitting at my table.

Then, I ask God to please sit at the table of my soul with Anger. You know what? He always sits in between us. *Always*. And he is kind to her. He wraps his arms around her, comforts her, and calms her.

I invite God into the parts of myself that he already knows. The parts of me that I am not gentle with. The parts of me that I fight against. The parts of me that had to develop in order for me to survive. And He is not surprised by them. He knows them intimately.

Instead of feeling threatened by these bullies, the healthier and stronger I become, I can see them for what they are. Anger is part of me, but she is not *me*. Anger has served a purpose in my unhealed and unhealthy self to protect me, to help me with something.

The healthy and healed version of me doesn't need the emotional or mental bullies to step in and get the job done anymore. They don't need to protect me or make decisions for me.

And when ugly memories assault my mind, I do something similar. I let myself have the memory, but instead of sitting there alone, I ask God to show me where he is. I ask him to be with me.

I make a mental note of where he is right now as I visit that memory, where I can actually see him. And I ask him what he is feeling and what he wants me to know.

Listen. If you do this and the words you hear are *anything other* than loving and encouraging, that's not God. God doesn't go into our pain with us and point the finger or shame. That's somebody else's voice. That's the voice of your enemy. He wants you to be terrorized by your memories, by your emotional and mental bullies. Your enemy wants you to be convinced that you deserved it, you brought it on, you will never heal, and this is all there is for you.

Your heart, mind, and soul are not meant to be a playground for shame and lies.

> *"They tried to bury us, they didn't know we were seeds."*
>
> –Dinos Christianopoulos

Be gentle with yourself. You are a seed. Seeds must break open in the dark before reaching the light and growing.

CRAZYMAKING

I can remember the first time I heard the term crazymaking. I was sitting in a therapist's office.

As I sat there, she looked at me, shook her head in disbelief, and said, "That's a recipe for crazymaking."

I didn't get it. At all.

Three months or so after cashing out the life insurance policy, he would throw it around in conversation and refer to it as *our* decision. It was what *we* thought was best.

What. What?!

What in the actual hell was he saying?

There was no "we" in that decision. *He* made that decision for me. He pushed me into it with zero regard for my heart or the relational backlash I would experience from my family.

I said nothing. I bit my tongue and shoved my thoughts deep into the back of my mind.

I suppose you could say gaslighters are creative at heart. They carry life-size paint brushes and sharpened pencils with plenty of extra erasers—like everywhere they go. They keep these tools with them.

This enables them to repeatedly recreate reality. They rewrite their past actions and fully expect you to see things exactly as they now see it.

The way that *you* recall things, your memory of events—however detailed it may be—has been slapped with a new coat of paint to match his memory. And that detailed account? No worries. He's written a new one for you.

He's not wrong. You must have remembered it wrong.

Doubt has started.

You doubt yourself and you look to him for the answers. You force yourself to acknowledge his version of truth instead of what you know to be true.

Your mind is being retrained. Your emotions are being relabeled. You are confused and he has positioned himself as your true north.

By definition, true north is the point of reference so you can reorient yourself in life's confusing situations. Are you following me on this? **The same person who is causing your confusion is positioning himself as the only one to steer you in the right direction.**

Not you. You can't do it. You thought you could do it. But you can't.

Only he can do it.

Right?

Is that right … Is it?

It must be. He loves you. You love him. It's fine. You're fine.

So why do you feel like a piece of gravel stuck between the treads on the bottom of a shoe? You don't belong there and yet you are stuck. Hemmed in on all sides.

Why did I feel like something wasn't quite right? Why wasn't I telling anybody?

The first year of marriage was supposed to be the honeymoon phase. I reasoned that my marriage didn't have that doe-eyed expression about it because we had dated for so long before taking our vows. We were just already comfortable. We didn't need to be sappy.

I would just settle for what we had. Other people told me that he was clearly gushy over me. Just because I didn't see it or feel it didn't mean it wasn't true. But it would be nice to hear how he felt.

I wasn't raised in a perfectly intact family unit. Nope. My parents had each been married multiple times. I have zero memories of my biological parents being kind to one another.

And yet, I received hugs and heard I love you regularly from my mom. I was comfortable with those three little words. They were a normal, everyday occurrence for me.

I had been waiting my whole life to say those three little words to my husband. It was good. It was right. It was natural.

But not for him.

I said those words freely. He didn't want me to say them. He made it very clear to me that saying "I love you" was not okay.

Love was expected. But saying it out loud, giving it voice? Well, that was not acceptable.

It was like this: Love me, but shut up about it.

I was supposed to shower him with love in a way that he could receive it. The key phrase in that thought being "in a way that he could receive it."

In the words of Hamlet, "aye, there's the rub."

Yep. I had a problem. Rather, he put a problem on me. *He put a problem on me.* And it was a problem that I was expected to solve.

When you do math problems, there are logical means to solve them. (Unless you're doing dadgum common core. If that's the case, well, my prayers are with you.)

To find the solution, there are steps to follow. There are formulas to learn. There are theorems. Some mathematical genius has gone before you, figured it all out, and laid out a plan for people to follow so they can find the solution, too.

That was not this.

There was no plan. And there was no solution.

No solution.

And yet I was expected to keep applying myself, applying my absolute best efforts into making him feel loved without speaking the words, "I love you."

Unless it was on the very extremely gold-plated-unicorn kind of rare day that he might actually tell me first. There was no rhyme or reason as to what made it a day that he might actually say those uncomfortable words.

And I was not to question it.

I tried and failed. I tried to make him comfortable with hearing the words that shall not be named and was reprimanded for trying to force it.

In my mind, it made no sense, but he had a perfectly acceptable reason as to why he didn't need to say it to me. His parents didn't say it.

Makes sense right? It made perfect sense why he was uncomfortable hearing and saying "I love you."

He had a reason and that was all there was to it. My need to hear it was not part of the equation. The need for it to be part of our marriage was unimportant. His need to not feel uncomfortable superseded all of it.

If I was a good and respectful wife, I would understand that and be mindful of it. If I was a good and respectful wife, I would know how to make him feel loved and wouldn't expect him to tell me he loves me.

I would figure out how to let him be and not expect anything in return. I wasn't allowed to expect anything from him. If I did, I was considered demanding and selfish.

Let's get this straight. He could expect things from me, but I could not expect things from him.

Does it make sense? No. His logic made no sense, yet I was expected to drink it in and accept it. Swallow his truth. No matter the taste it left in my mouth. No matter the feeling left in my body. No matter the thoughts tangled in my mind. No matter to my *self*.

My identity, my voice, my *self* ... it was all changing.

The Bible tells us when we get married that the two become one flesh. (Mark 10:8-10)

I reasoned that everything happening within me was all about becoming one flesh with him. The feelings and confusion must just be growing pains. After all, we were supposed to be in the process of becoming one mind and one flesh.

We were supposed to be thinking the same way, being like-minded. (Philippians 2:2)

He shared his thoughts and ideas frequently. They weren't something we discussed. They weren't something open for interpretation.

In his nearly infinite wisdom, his thoughts were blowing around me like dandelion fluff, ready to land at any moment, planting themselves in every part of me ... covering my head, my eyes, my arms, legs, back ... weighing down my shoulders ... invading the very air I was breathing.

I was no longer breathing my own air.

His thoughts, his very presence was occupying the air meant for my consumption.

It's like this ...

Imagine standing in a field of puffballs. Not just a field, a valley. You're surrounded on all sides by tiny balls of fluff, just waiting for a child to purse his lips and wish on every drifting seed.

As you stand there, you need to answer some important questions. You close your eyes to pause and think for a moment. When you open your mouth to speak, the wind picks up. Your words are stopped by fluff.

Opening your eyes, you see the fluff, thick in the air. You are surrounded by a fog of dandelion fluff. Reflexively, your arms begin to wave it away in an effort to keep it out of your nose and mouth. You blink it away as it reaches your eyelashes. You spit as it covers your lips.

Any thoughts, any words that were about to come out of your mouth have been overtaken by the fluff-filled air. No longer can you remember your own thoughts. You can't even see a way out of the valley.

At every turn, you're choking on the fog. It's in your mouth. It's in your nose. It's in your ears.

He is the fluff.

He is the wind.

And you? You are left standing in the storm of crazy. The storm of crazy that constantly swirls around you masquerading as truth, logic, wisdom, and love.

You are learning that you cannot find your way through it, you cannot see a way clear, so you must adapt and accept. You must learn to think in that fog, breathe in that fog, live in that fog.

For the love of Bear Grylls, you are in an extra special, real-life, gen-u-ine game of *Man vs. Wild* ... and you cannot escape your wilderness.

Welcome to life with a gaslighting narcissist and the crazymaking train that will be your ride through life.

Lucky you.

ACTIONS SPEAK LOUDER THAN WORDS

We didn't stay in the apartment long before deciding to get a house. At twenty-six, I was ready to have a place to call my own. I wanted to really put down roots and dream about a future together.

This house would be the place to build our family, to build our dreams.

I thought that being in a brand new house would be a new adventure, a new beginning.

Our little house was not on the prairie. It wasn't in the big woods. It was just a house. A plain-Jane, same-old-problems house. Conflict followed us down the road, turned into the driveway, walked up my sidewalk, and marched right through my front door.

I couldn't keep the house clean enough. I couldn't keep stuff organized.

That was not okay.

Nevermind that we were both working full time. His job was more physical than mine, so he had a reason to be more tired than me.

Whatever I did could always be improved upon. It was his duty to tell me all the ways I could be better. It was how a good husband loves his wife well. Must be true, he told me so. And my husband would never dream of telling me something to serve himself more than me.

I was determined to make our new, little house into a home while continuing to learn how to become an amazing wife.

People kept saying that conflict could bring people closer in a marriage. And the Bible says not to let the sun go down on your anger. (Ephesians 4:26) So, whenever we had a conflict, I wanted it to be resolved.

In my mind, that meant following him around the house when he was angry at me so we could resolve the conflict. I couldn't bear the thought of him being angry with me. It felt awful. It had to be resolved.

I remember following him throughout the house begging him to accept my apology for whatever I'd done to tick him off. My efforts were met with him completely ignoring me. I worked up my courage and found him in the bonus room.

He was not happy that I followed him.

My tear-filled eyes were met with a glare and unbridled anger. He shouted at me. Then, he stood up, turned around, and put his fist through the wall.

My whole body went rigid. I knew I was in trouble. I had gone too far.

Naturally, it was my fault because I wouldn't leave him alone. I wasn't showing him the respect he needed.

I went to bed, rolled over on my side, and skooched as far over to the edge as possible. I felt absolutely awful. Tears fell silently as I pretended to be asleep when he finally came to bed.

He flipped the lights on and continued with his earlier commentary on my behavior.

Still, I pretended to sleep.

We have a hole in our wall that will never be discussed. If we did mention the hole in the wall, it was to be discussed as something that we were both responsible for. Yep. He punched it, but I was responsible.

Essentially, he wanted me to know that I put a hole in our wall.

And when we asked our friend to help patch up the drywall, there was some sort of vague story presented as the truth.

Not once did he take full responsibility for his actions. He didn't need to. I carried the weight of it.

Gaslighters are great talkers.

That is part of their natural, narcissistic charm. They have great ideas and they love to talk about them. He says he is going to treat his wife like a queen and happily shares all the ways he is going to cherish her and put her first above himself. It's intoxicating really.

Gaslighters are great thinkers.

They can churn out some pretty fantastic ideas. When all of those precious, intoxicating things are said by a gaslighter, they mean them in the moment. And in those moments you believe them.

Here's the trick. Gaslighters say one thing and do something else entirely different.

He will tell you that you are beautiful and amazing. He will speak gently to you, hold your hand, touch your face, and compliment you. He will laugh at your jokes and steal glances at you from across a crowded room.

The Devil of *Then*

And then.

Then you get compliments coupled with constructive criticism. Your jokes and sense of humor are now seen as a reflection on him rather than being funny. And when he fails to be gentle, it is never because he isn't being gentle, it's because you drove him to that destructive behavior.

So even when his actions do not reflect his words, he has a rational, well-thought-out reason. There is nothing for you to say. No way for you to refute his words. He will convince you that his words make more sense than the thoughts in your head.

You and I both know that actions speak louder than words.

In my case, his actions would speak over and over and over.

Holes punched in walls and my chest of drawers, chairs broken, plates of food thrown at the ceiling or across the room.

I mean … Maybe he threw his plates gently? Sure, right.

To put it plainly, I was learning to pretend. I pretended his words were true. In order to not feel completely hopeless, I just flat out lied to myself. I felt like it was my only choice in order to emotionally survive.

That is how you survive in a marriage to a gaslighting narcissist. You develop your own survival mode and you hide there.

Yes. Hide to survive.

FAILURE TO ENGAGE

I wish I could tell you that I only followed him around the house that one time, but that would be a grievous understatement. It became a pattern for a while. I would follow him around begging for resolution to conflicts, and he would get irritated.

That should have prepared me for what happened next.

He was getting really sick of me. He believed I was a "lazy piece of shit." I was also deemed inconsiderate, selfish, a slob ... and a mistake. Actually, I was his "biggest mistake."

Now he had a reason not to tell me he loved me because he had decided that he was no longer sure that he loved me. And he completely stopped speaking to me.

Yes. I really felt like I was his queen. Every day. That crown fit so well that I barely noticed it.

Guess what made it even more special? The fact that we rode in to work together five days a week. Thirty minutes one way. Thirty minutes of complete silence. Thirty minutes of me fighting tears so I wouldn't show up to work looking exactly how I felt.

He would not speak to me no matter what I did or said.

This continued for five days.

Five days riding thirty minutes to work. Five days riding thirty minutes home. Five days of complete silence, and I never told anybody what was happening. I struggled and cried in complete isolation.

He was in control. I was at his mercy. Communication would only resume when he decided it would—exactly like when I would follow him around the house trying to resolve a conflict.

During any of our conflicts, he would decide when the conflict was over and when our relationship could move forward. And he would decide what happened during the conflict. That way, if the situation was ever brought up again, it would be spoken of in terms that were approved as truth by him.

And it was never ever okay to talk to others about the conflict unless I gave his approved version of the story. Oh. And of course, the story could only be shared with friends who he believed to be safe to tell.

Yeah. Umm … that didn't leave me with a lot of options.

I had to remain silent in the silence. I had to hold all of it inside myself. Tightly bound inside my heart and mind.

It also meant that I could not tell my family. I knew that I was supposed to leave and cleave. That's what the Bible said, and I took it very seriously. I was supposed to leave my father and mother and cling to my husband. (Ephesians 5:31)

At least that is what I was led to believe. It is most definitely a path that he wanted me to take.

It's almost unbelievable to think about how I began to keep things from my friends and family as a means to protect my husband within our marriage … while telling myself I was following God's plan.

Is it God's plan for us to be isolated?

Is it God's plan for us to walk through hard situations alone?

Is it God's plan for us to trust our husband's voice more than our own? More than God's voice?

No. No. Noooo.

Gaslighters isolate. They guide you into your isolation. They hold your hand and usher you into the space they're creating for you. The door to that space only opens in one direction, and it shuts behind you.

Those walls will go up around you and no one will know … not even you. The walls are not visible. The walls are not discussed. But the walls are absolutely understood.

They keep you trapped within and put a buffer between you and all the other voices that speak into your life.

Those damn walls are your boundaries. The lines you cannot cross.

You are learning how to behave. You are learning how to cope. You are learning how to be together *alone*.

And yet …

You have made plans. You are creating a life together. You are building dreams.

I was so proud of myself for being strong enough and wise enough to know that I could love enough for both of us. It might be painful, but I knew I could do it. I had been praying for this life.

I knew I walked into marriage with baggage from my parents' divorces. Experiencing multiple divorces in my parents' marriages had given me great examples of what I didn't want. Yep. I knew exactly what I didn't want.

I didn't want to quit. I didn't want to be hateful. I didn't want to be bitter. I didn't want to get a divorce.

Where did all of that leave me? It left me approaching marriage from a position of fear and determination … and with completely exposed vulnerability.

EXCUSES, EXCUSES

An old Italian proverb says, "The evil doer never lacks excuses."

Wow. I'd like to know which white-haired Italian came up with that little gem. And I also wonder if that person believes that children are evil. Lord knows that kids speak excuses over life like it's an actual language.

When we get older, we should outgrow the habit of making excessive excuses. In adulthood, we masquerade our excuses around as acceptable reasons.

Like that makes it okay. Yep. Just okie dokie.

Days roll on. And on. And on. And one day I woke up with my first baby. My first absolutely perfect baby boy.

His arrival seemed to take forever. My labor took over thirty-five hours. I was completely exhausted by the time my body was ready for pushing. Two and a half hours of pushing later brought my little guy into the world.

I was so in love.

We brought him home and I nursed him and changed all of his tiny diapers. At just five days old, I no longer had help with him. My husband went back to work. My mom went home. It was just the two of us.

I was scared. I was tired. And I was drowning in hormones and breast milk.

Three weeks later, we had visitors who came to see the first grandson. Our visitors fixed me dinner and wanted me to actually sit down and eat it. That would've been my first seated meal in weeks.

He was holding the baby while I ate. A few minutes into my meal, tiny boy began to fuss. My husband walked into the living room, glared at me, and angrily motioned for me to go to our bedroom.

When I got into the room, he thrust our newborn into my arms and began to tell me how selfish and inconsiderate I was for continuing to eat as our baby cried. I sat down and began nursing him.

He continued to rage at me in hushed tones, making sure that our guests would not hear him speaking to me. I fed our baby while crying and listening to his barrage of insults and accusations.

Then he grabbed the corner of our bed and lifted it up in the air as he continued on and on about how awful I was.

He was enraged.

It was as if he sucked every bit of air from the room and replaced it with smoke. You can't breathe in smoke. You can't see in smoke. And this smoke was completely paralyzing. It held me there.

I was trapped in the bedroom with him. Part of me was absolutely terrified about being in a room with him. The other part of me was desperate for them to hear what he was doing, come into our room, and make him stop.

They never did.

It was the first time I fantasized that someone would rescue me.

We walked out of the room forty minutes later and pretended like everything was fine. There was an obvious pretense. Nobody would address the tension we were ignoring. And I would spend the rest of the visit making sure I didn't take advantage of the visitors.

The visitors who had come to help.

It was clear that I wasn't allowed to let them help too much. I was supposed to take care of my newborn and play hostess. After all, he was working full-time and I had plenty of time to rest while I was sitting down breastfeeding.

Yes, I was responsible for all of the laundry, the meals, the diapers, and the cleaning of the house because, again, I was the one staying at home and he was the one who was working all day.

His mind never stopped. He was always thinking. So, he spent his days thinking and thinking and rationalizing and reasoning as to why he did just about everything.

He could back up all of those reasons with what he had learned from God. And who can argue with God? Nobody.

Naturally, he couldn't help with any of the stuff at home because his job made him more tired than other people. Not to mention that he was very tired because the baby was waking him up.

Did he ever get up in the middle of the night to change diapers or bring me the baby? No. Did he actually leave the bed? No. But *he* was tired, much more tired than I was.

He turned his excuses into reasons and brought God into his argument. I was to be thankful and have a positive attitude because I was blessed to stay home with our baby.

There was absolutely no reason that I could complain or be upset. None.

Only he had acceptable reasons for what he did.

Excuses, excuses.

Our playing field was not level.

He was above. I was below. That's how he wanted it. That's how it had to be.

There Is No Level Playing Field With a Gaslighting Narcissist

You see ... You can never ever be on a level playing field with a gaslighting narcissist. Not. Ever. You are meant to accept all of their excuses as viable reasons.

Just shut up and move on. That becomes your survival mantra.
It had certainly become my mantra.

And adding a new baby? Well, that basically meant more and more ways for me to fail and more opportunities for him to correct me.

He corrected my diaper changes, my breastfeeding, and my post-baby body. Of course, he did it all in the name of helping me.

I think that's when I began to tell myself, *I can't win.*

I ... cannot ... win.

A new baby was taking my time, my energy, and my focus. And that was not okay. Everything I did was wrong.

I was becoming a pro at course correcting. My feelings no longer needed to be expressed. They needed to be stuffed into a tiny little pouch. A manageable pouch that could be hidden away to fester in private.

Gaslighters have reasons for everything they do.

When you're on the receiving end, next to none of your reasons are acceptable. Your reasons will be considered excuses.

And your excuses are not valid. No. They are unacceptable.

You feel like everything you do is wrong. And according to his words and attitude, you have no reason to believe otherwise.

But you'll hang on and you'll keep plugging away because you are committed, you love him, and he throws in crumbs of encouragement to you.

Even though crumbs are not enough for the average person to live on, you pick them up and convince yourself it's a meal. Meanwhile, you pour yourself out for your family, just hoping he will be happy.

You are adapting to your surroundings. It's how you survive. You live in the land of blame. And every line you walk is a fine one.

In my home, if there was a mess, a diaper rash, or an accident, then it was because of something I did. There was no getting around it. Remember? No excuses.

I was not clean, not thoughtful, not considerate, and not safe. But I was blessed and so lucky to be staying home with our baby. It's true. He told me so.

FINGER POINTING

I was held responsible when our son fell down. I was responsible when he had a diaper rash. I was even responsible when he wouldn't take a bottle.

And do you know what else I became responsible for? A grown man's feelings of inadequacy. Frankly, I think I became responsible for everything that gave my husband a feeling he didn't like.

I stayed home with the baby while he worked. So, when I left the house to do anything, I had to fully prepare him. That meant cleaning the house first so he had no messes to deal with. I had to wash all the dishes, fix food, and write out any directions for him.

You see, he was babysitting for me. He was doing me a favor.

While most babysitters have been taught to clean up before the parents get home, that was my job, too.

After eating the food I made, he left the pots and pans for me to clean up. That only made sense because I was the one who had gotten them dirty.

I might not have had to pay him for watching his own child, but I was surely supposed to be openly thankful. Always thankful.

And always to blame.

When I got home, if that baby had cried and caused him stress, I would hear about it. If that baby didn't want to take a bottle, I needed to get home and deal with it. My evening plans were not important. I needed to hurry my selfish, inconsiderate self up and get home.

Should my sweet baby fuss during church or any other gathering and some other well-seasoned mama offer to take him out of my arms, it couldn't last. He wouldn't allow that. Uh-uh.

He would apologetically, yet heroically take our baby from their arms, hold on for a couple of minutes, and promptly put him in my arms. Then he would quietly hiss to me that I shouldn't be taking advantage of other people. He was ashamed and embarrassed of my typically self-ish and socially inappropriate behavior.

Y... O... U.

Me. My fault. My bad.

His fingers seemed to be pointed at me constantly.

When someone points his finger at you, they don't physically touch you, but you feel it deeply. Every point hurts, makes you flinch.

I inwardly flinched so often that I pretty much developed an emotional twitch. My coping skills game was in high gear. I was building walls around my heart and mind. Too bad those walls were not impenetrable.

I was in this horrible place of avoiding his criticism and irritation ... while simultaneously attempting to pursue living out my wedding vows.

Our relationship was on the struggle bus. I knew that I had come from a family of several broken marriages, so of course I was messing up. Of course, I couldn't possibly have known how to be a good wife.

He had been raised going to church. He had been raised with the same married parents in his home. He had the better example to follow and all the wisdom needed for a successful marriage.

I had gone to church, too. But, my parents hadn't stayed married in any of their marriages. And neither of my parents took me to church as a teenager. I did that all on my own. So, no parent was guiding me.

Once upon a time, I held fast to the belief that going to church on my own as a teenager had helped me to *own* my faith. It wasn't something passed on to me through family tradition or culture. I chose it. I *chose* to follow Christ.

That was a big deal to me.

Until it wasn't.

Until the day I began to believe that the leader of our home could hear God more clearly. He was supposed to be the spiritual leader and he repeatedly reminded me that he had the gift of discernment and wisdom.

The Devil's in the Doubting

Damn that doubt. My voice was not my own. The voice of God speaking to me was no longer to be trusted because it must first be filtered through him. Everything must be filtered through him.

Communication to a neighbor? Instructions to a handyman? Emails to church? Yeah. He needed to give his input to make sure I was representing him properly. Nevermind that I had a college degree and he didn't. I must have his help.

If I didn't get his input, then I was being completely inconsiderate, and his disappointment and contempt were palpable.

My words, my thoughts … were being redirected to what I thought was "becoming one flesh." It felt gross, but I had come to believe that was because I was a sinful person and selfish. It was supposed to be painful to become one with another person.

Right?

Even though it didn't feel right, I just kept convincing myself over and over and over that it was hard for me because I grew up in a broken home. It was going to get better because I was going to figure it out. I was going to keep praying, going to Bible studies, and learning from my mistakes.

IT'S NOT ME, IT'S YOU

"You don't like me. You don't even act like you like who I am as a person," I told him.

I was determined to put my heart out there and be honest, be vulnerable. Vulnerability means a closer relationship. It means intimacy.

I wanted intimacy.

"That's not true. I don't like your behavior. Everybody hates other people's sin. How can you expect me to like your sin?" he replied, looking at me like I was laced up in a straight jacket.

Okay. Well, great. That didn't make me feel any better. And I didn't feel heard or understood. That was becoming a theme.

"I don't feel like you even love me. You don't say it. You get weird when I say it. And you only touch me when you want sex," I continued, hoping he could hear me and understand.

"Well, I'm sorry you feel that way. That's not true. I've never said that," he replied with a slight smirk, staring into my eyes. And he began another "helpful husband" lesson in teaching me how my behavior could be improved so that I could be less sinful and communicate with him more effectively.

Because I couldn't communicate. In fact, I was a terrible communicator. Just ask him. He knows. He knows everything.

No compassion. No understanding. No validation for my thoughts or feelings. Just more helpful tips spoken for my betterment.

That's right. That is exactly how it works. *It's not them, it's you.*

It Had to Be You

When the fight rises up within you, when your identity begs for the light, when your voice screams into a vacuum … You will squelch it. The spirit within you that used to point you in the direction you should go will be stifled.

And you will be the one to stifle it.

Because if you don't stifle it, you will be forced to deal with the consequences. You will be forced to face truths that no one else seems to believe, including you.

If you could just find the right words, make the right cleaning schedule, have the right body, cook the right way, parent in a better way … then things would change. Then he would be pleased. Then you could actually please him and that would make you both happy.

It's not him, it's you.

You need to change. *You* imagined the attitude. *You* remembered it wrong. *You* made him do it. *You* are to blame.

So, you wear his labels. You believe his lies. You eat his shit.

How is it? For real. How does it taste knowing that you have been not only chewing but also swallowing every bit of shit he spews at you?

You cannot live on a diet of shit. You can survive. You can cope. You can exist. But you cannot *live*.

Is that what you want? Is that how you want to spend your days?

I went to listen to a special speaker at my church one evening. The guy speaking was a man who knew me. He was a leader of several small groups and counseled people regularly.

This night was partially designed to teach us about different personality types and how they played out in real life.

I'm the type of person who doesn't mind volunteering to be on stage. So when he asked for people to come play the various roles, I raised my hand. Wouldn't you know it? He picked me.

We all stood on stage together as he doled out our various personality roles to play. When he got to me, he announced my label—*loudly*. Keep in mind that we are at a church meeting.

"You are the shit eater," he said, with a little too much purpose. "Shit eaters stay on their knees with their mouths gaping open to swallow the shit that is fed to them."

In my role, I had to get on my knees, tilt my chin up, and open my mouth while another person pretended to shovel all of her crap into my mouth.

How appropriate.

If he only knew the absolute depth of truth to my role. He thought he knew, but he didn't. Nobody knew. How could they? I never told the whole truth to another person. I couldn't even tell myself the truth.

After all, it was all my fault. It wasn't him, it was me.

I mean … Do they make Tide for brains? Because mine was fully being washed in all of *his* words and thoughts. My husband. His words and thoughts scrubbed and polished away my own thoughts, washing me anew with his replacement ideas, principles, values … I was to think like him. That's what he considered being like-minded.

We are not what we eat.

You are not what you have choked down. You are more.

Are you hearing me? No. Are you *listening?* You can hear me all day long and let the words go in one ear and out the other. I want you to listen. I want you to believe and know in the depth of who you are that you are meant to live.

In our culture we talk a lot about survivors. We hear podcasts on victims and their survivors. We see the latest documentary on the victims of horrible abuse. We know that being punched in all of the places where bruises won't show is evil. And we think to ourselves, *That is not me. I don't have it that bad.*

And we are suddenly thankful that our bodies are not terrorized by fists, belts, or broken bottles. We are so thankful that our lives are not being threatened. We focus on gratitude and having an attitude of thankfulness.

Yes. Yesss. A right attitude on your part will help. Surely, being thankful for everything you have will go a long way.

Now, we're comparing our situation to the person who was bludgeoned to death. Our problems are nothing compared to that. Good grief. What on earth could we possibly have to complain about or question?

You are not like one of those victims. You are not surviving a near-death experience. You're totally alive. You're fine.

Of course you are.

You have a husband who pays the bills. He goes to church. He can even be super fun. You married a man with great ideas about the future.

That's what you'll focus on. *What's that Bible verse that tells us what to think? Something about whatever is lovely and noble ... and praiseworthy?*

I read blogs on gratitude. I prayed to be a better wife. I asked friends to pray for me to be a better wife. And after he would rage at me, I would cry silently and recite that Bible verse to myself, desperate to change my focus.

*"And the peace of God, which transcends all understanding, will guard your hearts and your minds in Christ Jesus. Finally, brothers and sisters, **whatever** is true, **whatever** is noble, **whatever** is right, **whatever** is pure, **whatever** is lovely, **whatever** is admirable—if anything is excellent or praiseworthy—think about such things."* Philippians 4:7-8 NIV

I will focus on other things. I just need to get my mind right. I can do this. If I focus on the negative, nothing will get better.

That's what I would tell myself. My well-meaning friends would give me their favorite verses and books on marriage and being a Godly wife.

In the meantime, I would keep this to myself. Nobody was beating me.

Do you know what part of that verse I never ever, not one cotton-picking time, let sink in? "Whatever is TRUE."

Yeah. That tiny little part about truth.

When you are being gaslighted, telling the truth is an elusive thing. You think you know the truth. You could swear up and down that you know exactly what was said, what was done, and how it all made you feel.

But then he speaks.

His voice dominates your own. His version of truth throws a blanket over your ridiculous claims. His eyes tell you that you're crazy, you're losing it. *You* don't know the truth. *He* knows the truth.

Sometimes, he isn't even there, yet his voice is louder than your own. His voice has become such a driving force in your life that you filter all of your thoughts through the man who has filled your mind with himself.

Gaslighting whispers into the most-hidden corners of your mind and tells you that you are not okay.

Meeting You Where You Are

People will think I quit.

They won't understand.

I'll be a total hypocrite for all the years I spent talking about the sanctity of marriage and that I would never ever get divorced.

Other people have it much worse than I do.

They're going to think I'm making this up.

My kids are going to suffer so much.

Those are just a few of the thoughts that ran through my mind over and over when I walked away. I'm guessing you're having a few of these, too. So, let me tell you what I know …

People will think whatever they choose to think and you can't stop them. Period.

People who don't want to know won't even try to understand. Those are not your people. And many people will never understand. They can't. They haven't experienced your life.

Are you really a hypocrite? Your spouse broke the covenant with God long before today when he chose to continue to abuse you. If you still believe that marriage can be a really good thing, then I'd venture to say that you're not a hypocrite. You're a daughter of the King who remembered that her Daddy doesn't want her to be abused for the rest of her life.

Other people may have it worse than you, but that doesn't make your situation okay. Hear me loud and clear on this: **Prolonged psychological abuse can damage you in ways that are far more lasting than a physical beating.** That isn't my opinion, it is a fact.

The damage of unhealed psychological trauma reaches into the future of your health emotionally, mentally, and physically—even *without a hand* ever being laid on you.

You may not need to get a divorce. Maybe your spouse will truly repent and get help. That would be amazing. I would love, love, love that for you.

But.

What is your present reality? You must be realistic about what your past and present reality show you to be true. That is what you base your decision on. You cannot trust your safety to what you hope *might* happen.

Yep. People may think you're making it up. It'll hurt. Yes, that's *more* hurt. And it really sucks. Those are not your people! Even if they have seemed like your people for years, they are no longer your people.

Believe me, I have plenty of new people. And I also have plenty of people who surprised me with their encouragement and support because they knew something wasn't right.

You need people who can walk alongside you. Your new people may be in an online group. They don't have to be physically present to walk with you emotionally.

As for your children suffering more … They are already suffering. Every time they watch or listen to you being shamed, controlled, or raged at, they suffer. Our kids literally feel it when their mom is in pain. It scares them. It hurts them. And for older kids, it angers them.

Will they suffer if you walk away? Yes. But you can create space for healing! You create an environment for them to take a deep breath. Your kiddos have been holding their breath for their entire little lives, just waiting for something bad to happen.

You cannot take away all of their suffering. You can't insulate them from hurt and sadness. You can't control how their dad will behave. But you have the power to make *your* space one that feels safe.

This is when all of us had the room for our anxiety to come to the surface. It meant not sleeping and panic attacks and lashing out.

It's scary. It makes you question what you've done. And it's okay.

Think of a pressure cooker or your Instant Pot. The contents inside are under pressure the entire time that lid is on. But you can't keep the lid on forever. If you do, you can't get to the good stuff inside.

So, you learn to use the vent. You give that steam a place to go. And then you can take the lid off.

But kids don't know this, and frankly, you don't either. I sure as heck didn't know. We limped along together. And even in our limping, I was and am their safe space.

If I let all the voices in my mind dictate my choices, I'd still be in my closet. I'd still be driving around crying on Mother's Day. And I definitely wouldn't be writing a book or leading other women.

My trauma would be leading me around by the nose. (I mean, sometimes my trauma still tries to put a ring in my nose and yank me around!)

Your trauma will masquerade as the voice of reason. Your trauma will parade around like your hero coming in to rescue you from making an uncomfortable decision.

Healing is not comfortable.

Growing is not comfortable.

Removing the chains of abuse is not comfortable.

But it is better.

It is better to heal, to grow, and to be out of an abusive environment. It is better to trust yourself. It is better to love yourself. And it is better to be safe.

When your mind isn't safe, you are not safe.

When your child's mind isn't safe, she isn't safe.

My road isn't easy. But I have the space to heal. My kids have the space to heal. And I am walking in the light at the end of my tunnel.

THE COST YOU KNOW

You know. Some part of you knows that something is not right. But if you listen to that part of yourself, if you focus on it, nothing good will come of it.

That's what you know.

What you know for sure, what you have learned, is that what he says must be seen as the truth. If you don't see things his way, there is a cost. And that cost will be paid by you.

If he says what you believe just isn't true ... If he looks at you like you're crazy ... If he stares into your face with that look of contempt ... You know the cost. You know there is a price to pay for daring to disagree, for grimacing, for showing any sign that you aren't listening, for giving any hint that you think what he's saying is not 100% believable.

Plates will be thrown against the ceiling, leaving pasta and sauce stuck to it as evidence. Evidence that will remain there.

Plates will be slung across the room with syrup splattering those curtains you spent hours making only to be told he doesn't like them. The syrup will remain there until a crusty arrangement of spots is indelibly formed.

Plates will be slammed on the table with so much force that it shuts the mouths of everyone seated there and holds them hostage in silence while the plate chips and cracks.

And your body? Your body is the vessel for containing all of the tension, all of the fear, hurt, and loneliness that is thrown around the room. You will shut your mouth and you will carry it all. Otherwise, there will be another price to pay.

You know the cost because you live the cost.

You know something is wrong but you can't think about it. You can't think about it because you're too busy maintaining a facade of calm. You can't think about what is so painfully wrong because you are mentally sifting through expectations and duties.

You know something is wrong, but you have learned that thinking for yourself is unacceptable and frankly, after years of gaslighting, you have forgotten how to think for yourself. How can a person figure out what is wrong when you no longer feel the capacity to even allow yourself to reason?

So, How Many Years Has It Been?

You have been living in a state of confusion. You have been questioned. You have been spoon fed lies. You have been belittled. You have been blamed.

Has it been so long that you actually believe it?

I sure did. It seemed safer that way. My mind was in self-protection mode all the time. My heart had gone into hiding. All of that fight inside of me was buried.

I knew that a car ride to church could be derailed within minutes if he got pissed off on the way. It could mean he turned around and went home while I took the kids by myself. That meant sitting in service alone and worrying about how pissed off he'd be when we got home.

I can't even begin to count the number of times I showed up at a family event with my kids, trying to hide the fact that he'd decided not to come because he was mad about something. Of course, I was supposed to present myself as though everything was normal or that it was my fault he hadn't come.

Living my life meant knowing how to pretend like a champ.

My fourth baby was nine days old when it was the perfect time for a meltdown. Not a meltdown for me, of course, because that wasn't allowed. Nope. Carrying that fourth baby and taking care of three other children under the age of six was really hard for him to watch.

Yes, *watch*. He didn't change diapers. He had decided that he wasn't really good at it and that he would just let me do it like 99% of the time. He also never washed any of the laundry that piled up for a newborn, three kids, and two adults. And getting up all night nursing the baby was really hard on him as well because it woke him up.

All the work I was doing had just absolutely exhausted him and caused him an excessive amount of stress. And nine days after I gave birth to our baby, he couldn't contain it anymore.

So, he started in.

"You are a slob. This is ridiculous. Why do we need three spatulas? Nobody needs three spatulas. Why can't you keep these containers organized? Just put things back where they go!!

"You're a hoarder. You hoard things. We don't need this many cups. We have no reason to have plastic cups and glasses. You have a problem …"

He continued on his rampage as he slammed kitchenware into a trash can. He continued filling it up with serving dishes, storage containers, utensils … All the while yelling at me and telling me I was a hoarder.

Nine years into marriage and I had been well trained. I knew that leaving the room was not an option. I was expected to stand there holding my newborn while he let me know how irresponsible and immature I was, how my lack of consideration for others in the way I lived was ruining the lives of those around me.

When I opened my mouth to dare defend myself, it was clear that my words only served to fuel his fire, fuel his reasoning for labeling me as crazy. How could I possibly see things any other way than the way he sees?

I would be reminded again that I was only to think for myself when it was convenient for him. He was allowed to change the terms at any moment. And I was supposed to go on about my day like a normal lesson had just been taught. A lesson that should fill me with gratitude.

So I did. I pretended like nothing happened. I ignored the fact that he'd thrown away countless items from our wedding registry. I would turn my mind off and force the thoughts about what had happened right on into the far, dark corners of my mind to keep company with all the other things to never be named.

It was the price I would pay. It was the cost I knew so very intimately.

I had trained my mind to just keep expanding over and over to contain the feelings and thoughts that were not acceptable in my marriage. It's amazing how much a person can keep shoveling into the dark space. And they like it there.

Secrets love the dark.

They can have a mind of their own in the dark. They grow claws and hooks in that darkness. Secrets bury pieces of you with them and their hooks grab tightly and refuse to let go. It's the price of secrets.

It's not just that you're keeping a secret though, is it? It's that you're keeping all of these secrets and you have to pretend that there are no secrets. Everybody in the house must pretend that they know nothing about secrets.

And when you have kids, you teach them how to pay the price without understanding the cost.

Yeah. I did that. I taught my children to stay silent, to pretend.

Survival mode is a real thing for me. Survival mode is a real thing for my kids.

SURVIVAL MODE

W hen you've been living with a gaslighter, every day is a game of survival. It's how you manage to muddle through the moments of wishing you could disappear and just stop existing. But you can't do that. You don't get to disappear.

You must be invisible. You cannot disappear.

You have responsibilities. So, so many responsibilities. And you must handle them all. You must keep all of the plates spinning. Wash the clothes, wash the dishes, wash the toilets, wash the sinks, wash the babies.

You already know you can't keep him happy, so you look for ways to make him temporarily happy. Temporary happiness means that there will be bits of kindness thrown your way. And you are used to scraps. You've been surviving for years on the scraps.

Survival mode also means self-protection mode.

In my marriage, my heart and mind were not safe, so I would shield them. I would avoid conflict as much as humanly possible.

I remember listening to men preach from the pulpit about conflict bringing marriages closer. I remember ladies standing in front of Bible studies and insisting that stepping into conflict leads to deeper intimacy. Books had pages and pages of instruction on the blessings of conflict.

What a crock.

None of these people know what it's like to step into conflict within my marriage. None of them have an ounce of empathy for a woman stepping onto the battlefield disguised as a simple marital conflict.

Not one of those people knew what it cost me to engage in conflict with my husband.

And it cost me too much.

Engaging in conflict within my marriage meant walking blindfolded into a minefield.

I must speak, or I was accused of not listening. Yet I was not to speak at the wrong time because speaking before he had finished his discourse was completely disrespectful. I was meant to listen attentively until he allowed my response.

And that response? Well, that response could absolutely under no circumstances resemble anything of a defense. If I were to defend myself after listening to several minutes of his revelation of my sin, then I would be accused of being incapable of recognizing my own depravity, of lying to myself, of lying to him, of arguing.

"You always argue," he'd spit while narrowing his eyes and glaring as if I were the devil. "You don't know how to contend without arguing. You're the reason why the kids argue. Nobody else would ever put up with you the way I do ..."

I wish I could say that it stopped there, but it never did—especially if I made the mistake of trying to answer all of his accusations.

"I can't say anything to you without you getting defensive! What is wrong with you?! You need help," he'd yell.

And I would stand there, eyes down, shutting him out as much as possible without leaving his presence. Leaving his presence was seen as an act of defiant disrespect and would lead to more insults.

And my goal was survival.

I was absolutely not going to walk out of this marriage. I was going to honor my wedding vows. So what if I wasn't really living?

I was still alive. I was taking care of my kids. I was creating a bunker around my heart. And I sure as shit knew how to survive behind that bunker. Duck for cover. Dodge his bullets. Just survive.

Send my kids to their rooms before he exploded. Get busy cleaning no matter how tired I was. Teach my kids to clean up so he would have less to rage about. Teach them to shut up so he would have one less thing to accuse them of.

Clean it up. Shut your mouth. Survive. And smile.

He was completely disgusted with me ... and he wanted me to believe it was my fault, that I caused whatever problem it was. After all, it's better to live on your roof than to be stuck inside a house with an argumentative wife. I mean, that's how he used Proverbs 21:9. So, that's how I applied it to myself.

A teeny tiny part of me didn't believe him and was questioning what he said.

But that part was quickly silenced by the voices. *Make this marriage work. I am not a good wife. He was raised in a Christian home. I need to be a good wife. Who wants to live with someone like me who isn't a great wife? Just shut up and learn to be more respectful. If I could just be better, then he'll be nicer.*

And on and on. The voices would not shut up and any whisper of my own voice was long gone.

Just shut up and survive.

THE LYING GAME

Words are like weapons.

"You're a liar."

"I know you're lying to your friends about me."

"I know you're telling your family lies about me."

And as the kids kit about the age of four, there were more targets to hit ...

"You're a liar ... just like your mom."

I cannot begin to count the number of times my children have heard those words. And like their mother, they eventually learned to just stand there and be silent amid the onslaught of questions.

Ohhh, the questions. Any incident, any sibling argument was met with questions. Question upon question upon question, all of which already have answers because he's decided the answers before he asks.

That's how it works. Right?

Something happens. Could be a look he doesn't appreciate, an unapproved tone, a messy room, a kid screaming. Whatever it is, it's time for his intervention.

So, whatever the situation, he immediately makes his presence known.

"What's going on?" he asks.

And whoever is standing there tries to answer. If you show any sign of fear, it's because you did something wrong and you're a liar. If you hesitate, you must be lying. If you look away, it's because you cannot face the truth.

As the child stands there with their father towering over them, the fear is palpable. They are desperately trying to answer his questions, but their own words are being used against them.

It's a trap.

By the time each of my kids was in kindergarten, they knew what was coming. They knew that the questions were coming, and they knew that they had to answer … but no matter what they said, they would not give the right answer.

It was a trap. My kids knew that they must agree with whatever their daddy says, or they would be in even more trouble for lying. This trap meant the only winner *ever* was their dad. He was the decider of truth.

And that is exactly how it would be.

You see, he deemed himself as discerning. Period. Him. Not me. Not our kids. *Him.* He was the only one in our home who could discern the truth in every situation. *Every situation.*

This self-acknowledged truth even applies if there are witnesses. The witnesses will also be questioned. This applies to adult witnesses. Nobody is as reliable as he is, even in his absence. So, every witness walks away feeling completely disregarded.

You Are on His Game Board

There is a reason for that. You *are* disregarded. You have been entered in a game. You don't know the name of the game. But you learn the rules and the players very quickly.

The first rule of the game is that he wins. Whichever way you move on the board, he wins. Whatever number on the dice you roll, he wins.

The second rule of the game is that you must keep playing. You are not allowed to stop playing the game until he allows it. You can try to bow out, but he won't let you. And remember, he wins.

The third rule is that he makes up the rules. And his rules change according to his purposes. Speak up. No, shut up. Be sad. But stop crying. Agree with whatever he says, but don't lie. And always remember: *You can't win. Only he can.*

It's one thing to find yourself trapped in a game with a gaslighting narcissist who uncontrollably rages … but it's a whole different level of gaming when you witness your children trying to survive a game that they will never ever win.

"Just tell me the truth," he says.

"I am telling the truth, dad," my child replies for the umpteenth time.

"There is no way you are telling me the truth ..." he replies, getting angrier and more disgusted.

As the mom, I would attempt to intervene. I wanted to bring a voice of reason. I wanted my kids to know that they were not alone, that they were going to be okay.

It was about nine years in to our twenty-year marriage when he started shutting the door in my face, keeping me from their rooms while he disciplined them in all of his grandiose wisdom and godly instruction. (Cough, cough, gag.)

Yes. He *shut the door in my face.*

"You are making me escalate!"
"You are not supporting me!"
"You always make me the bad guy!"

As he grabbed their little arms and yanked them into their bedrooms, I was not allowed to follow unless I could find a way to make him feel supported in the middle of his fit of rage. (Fit is a better word for it, don't you think?)

So, I would walk in and speak in low, gentle tones.

"Hey. This is not the man you want to be. This is not the kind of dad you want to be ..."

"Ohhh, SHUT. UP," he would growl.

My voice would turn to pleading as I recognized the terror on my babies' faces. And yet I knew if I did not leave, he would purposely get worse and take it out on the kids. Doors would be slammed, a blind rage would follow.

I could not win.
My kids could not win.
We all knew it.

I'm not sure how many times we have all lied over the years because he refused to believe the truth. The only way to stop the badgering was to admit to something that wasn't true. So, no matter what, when you are married to a covert narcissist, you are a liar.

MONKEY SEE ... MONKEY DON'T

A gaslighting narcissist is super fun to parent with. I mean ... the marriage is already like living with a pop-up thunderstorm, so why not add several kids to the mix? Sure. It makes for a bigger audience to listen to their life lessons.

The life lessons ... Lord have mercy. Those lessons are as easy to swallow as a pinecone. Good times.

Most narcissists are going to be total pros when it comes to gaslighting. They don't have to take lessons because they do it naturally. When you view life from your own perspective on a constant basis, it's pretty easy to do.

If your situation is at all like mine, then using Google to find all the traits of a narcissist have left you pretty confused. So instead, look up "closet narcissist" or "covert narcissist" or "covert passive-aggressive narcissist." Your jaw will probably drop open as lights pop on in your mind.

But no matter the type of narcissist, the gaslighting remains. The level to which you experience it may be different. The tactics may be slightly different. And honey, if your abuser (yep, I meant to use the word "abuser") is a Christian, your gaslighting is probably going to be even harder to recognize and come to terms with.

One of the Bible verses that my abuser liked to use frequently is about gentleness.

Does any part of what you've read so far describe a man who models gentleness in his home? Well, just imagine that I have only told you about the first twelve years of a relationship that lasted almost a quarter of a century.

I was in deep. So very deeeeep.

I loved that he wanted us to use Bible verses in our home. Me, too! Me, too! To a woman who loves Jesus and wants a family who follows Him, this is a really good thing.

Until the verses become weapons of manipulation, tools of shame, and a means of silencing.

"Let your gentleness be evident to all. The Lord is near." (Philippians 4:5) He talked about this verse frequently as he spoke of his desire to be a more gentle man. (He was allowed to talk about his anger, but nobody else was allowed the privilege of confronting him about it. And I mean *no one*.)

When our kids would get upset and lose their tempers, he would remind them of this verse and tell them to keep their composure. In other words, they were supposed to be gentle and self-controlled.

If they got upset and lost their tempers, you'd better believe a consequence and a lecture was coming. Did you know it's possible to lecture a five year old for fifteen minutes and fully expect them to pay attention? To expect a little boy to hold eye contact every time you give a lecture?

It is totally possible. I watched it happen for over sixteen years. The lectures got longer with age. And once again, I was not allowed in the room during these lectures. But when I needed to have a talk with our kids? That door had better be open and he had better be included.

Do as I say, not as I do.

That man had a lot to say. About everything. Talk, talk, talk. Lecture, lecture, lecture. And everybody was expected to listen with gratitude for the life lessons we were being given.

He especially liked to give life lessons in the middle of a game. Super fun. Imagine playing outside, just a simple game like four square. That game starts out with laughter and siblings picking at each other in fun.

Then he steps into the game.

The mood shifts quickly. The child who struggles more with the game receives zero grace and compassion, but instead gets lessons on honesty, trying harder, and character. Meanwhile, the other sibling who doesn't like to be competitive with her dad is getting a life lesson on playing to win because that's what God tells us to do.

Fun. Yes, we could really feel the love of Jesus. Thanks, dad.

Unfortunately, his actions and reactions were screaming much louder than his lessons. His actions were making all of his words impossible to respect. And do you know what that means for kids? It means they are watching a man who loses his temper and rages about once a week.

It means they were learning how to respond to situations in their lives by overreacting and then being scared of what happens when they mess up. And then, getting in trouble for repeating behaviors they watched him model. That's not a recipe for success.

And if that wasn't bad enough, quite often his raging fits would happen after going to church in the morning, telling us everything he learned and how he was going to apply it, and then his mood would shift by late afternoon. He became noticeably edgy.

Just like clockwork, his actions would no longer line up with his words. That's a gaslighting move right there.

Pie Crust Promises

In third grade, I learned about a pie crust promise. It's a promise made that is easily broken.

Narcissists know all the right things to say, all the pretty, flowery, impressive words to use. They are full of charm. And their natural propensity for gaslighting means they are experts at making promises … but they suck at keeping them.

And you know what? They don't have to keep their word. You cannot make a gaslighter keep their word unless you have irrefutable proof of exactly what they said. Irrefutable proof would need to be in the form of a video recording.

No, I'm not kidding.

They need to see themselves making the promise. Otherwise, you might've twisted their words. You might've misheard them. You might just be making it up … after all, you are a liar. It would be just like you to make it up.

But ... if you were to record them, that would be a breach of trust. That would be disrespectful. That would be sinful and worthy of a consequence.

Here's a life lesson for you. You can't hold a gaslighter accountable for their words or actions. Only the gaslighter is allowed to hold others accountable. Accountability is not a two-way street for a gaslighting narcissist.

I knew better than to attempt to hold him accountable. And although he told me he wanted me to be his helpmate and that being his helpmate was my job as his wife, I could never quite do it right. I was supposed to help point him to Christ and help him be the man he was created to be.

But. Umm ... It's suuuuper hard to be a helpmate when honesty is unacceptable. It's hard to be a helpmate when you never seem to use the right tone or the right words, and you most certainly never speak at the right time.

Gaslighting has no room for you to succeed. It only leaves room for them to succeed. Your gaslighter gets to say whatever hateful, crappy thing he wants in the name of "helping" you and your children.

Gaslighters get to point out the flaws of all your family members, but you must bite your tongue when it comes to their family.

Gaslighters get to rage and completely lose their marbles and then act like nothing ever happened.

Gaslighters get to blow up your day, blow up your schedule, blow up your plans and you are expected to accept it with a good attitude.

Everything a gaslighter does is accompanied by a litany of rationalizations for their behavior and it is understood that questioning those rationalizations is unacceptable.

Do you know what happens when you question a gaslighter? When you respond with information that contradicts them?

YOU are crazy.
YOU can't see straight.
YOU are incapable of understanding.
YOU are arguing.
YOU are being abusive.
YOU are being a narcissist.

Not him. Never ever him.

And don't you dare try using his own words on him. Don't you dare try using one of his tactics. No ma'am. This will only bring his wrath. And once again, you will be the sinful, argumentative wife.

You cannot win.
Your children cannot win.

Monkey see ... monkey don't.

I DON'T MATTER

Eighteen years into marriage, there was one place I could be alone. One place I could put things wherever I wanted. One place I could eat chocolate cake or let the tears flow.

The one place I could be totally honest … was my closet.

At this point, my extended family barely recognized me. My mom would leave my house and cry on her drive home because she was so fearful and worried about what my life was like. My friends were gently throwing out phrases like "emotional abuse," "verbal abuse," and "too controlling."

I'd been to six therapists and church counselors. I had talked to pastors, Bible study leaders, and community group leaders. I was begging for help.

I walked into every therapy session just hoping somebody would finally tell me what was wrong with me. He told me I was a terrible wife. He made sure I knew I was the one who was damaged and needed help. He made sure I knew nobody else would want me.

I sat there and waited for them to tell me all the things I could change to be the wife he needed.

One of them actually looked at me, breathed out something like a cross between a scoff and a stifled cackle, and said, "You sound like an abused wife." I remember being horrified and denying it immediately.

Yeah, dude. That was really funny.

Every marital therapy session was a new resource for him. Every church small group teaching about the human heart was a new means for finding lessons to teach me. (Never mind that I was leading my own groups on those subjects.)

Any lesson that he could take and apply to me, he did. Any sermon he could listen to and apply to my life, he did.

Meanwhile, my small group people were telling me they hoped I would find my voice, which went right over my head. I totally didn't get it. I genuinely had no idea what that even meant. And they were telling me I should be leading other women.

Foolishly, I mentioned that I had been invited to lead small groups. He made sure to let me know that I would need to be very careful when I lead those groups because I had so much of my own junk to work on.

Narcissists can take information from situations and rewrite it into a story that suits their own narrative.

Once they've done this you'll know. Believe me, you will know ... because they'll use their narrative to gaslight.

I lost track of the number of times I held it together until I could shut my closet door, lay on the floor, cry without restraint, and scream into a pillow. The anguish within me was almost unbearable.

I had been burying pieces of myself over and over. Holding the very core of *who I am* captive within my mind and body was destroying me. He had spent the last two decades remaking me in his image.

All of my thoughts, my tasks, my actions, had to be filtered through my mindscape of his approval or disapproval. One thing I had learned for sure by eighteen years of marriage was this:

I do not matter.

I didn't. I absolutely did not matter.

That's when I decided to make myself own that version of reality. So, I grabbed a pencil, went into my closet, and wrote myself a reminder. "I do not matter."

In the next months, I would write those words over and over. The pencil marks served as a reminder that no matter what I said, no matter what I did, no matter how much I went out of my way to please him, *I did not matter.*

My voice did not matter.

It was as if my words were made of dust. They left my mouth but made no impact. And when they did land, they were easily brushed away.

I was no longer sure of who I was. And as for my voice, well, I'm not sure I would have recognized the sound of it. I had been shutting myself down for so long, trying to keep the waves in my home from drowning me.

His voice was the one that mattered. His thoughts. His words. His ideas. His dreams.

Sure … mine got an honorable mention, but they weren't worth pursuing. Whenever I pursued something, it was in the way. It was distracting me from my responsibilities in the home. It was seen as my idol.

Let me rephrase.

If I did something that made me happy and lit a spark in me, *he decided* I was not keeping our family as a priority, I was slacking in my duties, I was causing problems, and it (whatever it was at the time) had become my idol.

This put him in the position of pointing out my sin, of helping me. This "help" fed his self-righteousness and allowed him to rationalize his treatment of me. All of his explanations and rationalizations were expected to be received as the better way of doing things, of seeing things.

His way. Period.

Are you seeing this clearly? Are you following what was happening to me?

Of course you are. It's so much easier to see it when it is happening to someone else. It's possible to look at the situation and see that gaslighters are always shifting the sand they put beneath your feet disguised as solid ground. They are always grabbing the rug and pulling it out from under you, then blaming you for tripping.

You are the entertainment for his party. And he decides what you'll do, what you won't do, what you'll believe and what you won't, when you go or when you stay. And he decides when, why, and if you matter.

Know why?

Because you have been groomed to respond to him. He's been training you. Without hesitation, you immediately silence yourself and give his voice priority.

And you'll do nothing about it. You know the price for removing him from your thought process. You know the price for allowing your kids to have a voice.

So, you continue acting the part of the marionette while he directs your strings. You watch as your children step onto the stage and play their part along with you. And you tell yourself over and over that you are protecting them. You are keeping them safe.

Meeting You Where You Are

Today, I know that I matter. I know that I exist to be more than an emotional whipping post, a cook, and a cleaner.

I am a mother. But I am not just a mother.

I work. I am self-employed. I am raising my kids with very minimal help from their father. And we are all okay. My kids are in therapy. My kids are honor students.

I bought a house. I drive an old car. I bought new furniture. I don't have any curtains. But I love my new bedspread.

There are great things and meh things. Life certainly *looks* different. But I've learned that your life can look very different on the outside but feel the same inside your heart and mind.

When my circumstances changed, I had to make a choice to change my mind. My mind had to be rewired. My thoughts had to be rerouted.

When I realized that my thoughts were not my own, it meant consistent work to find my own thoughts. Yes. I basically had to go on a hunt for my mind. (Brings new meaning to "lost my mind," doesn't it?!)

For me, the first step was telling the truth. No more hiding. No more pretending. And I had to find people who could actually hear that truth, people who could handle it.

Not everyone can handle (or believe) my story. Not everyone is meant to be a part of my journey as I move forward. But the people who can stand alongside me and look me in the eye when I can barely stand my own reality—those are the right people.

I didn't find my buried voice all in one fell swoop. If you think of your inner voice like a little girl who's been hiding from danger for years, you might understand why she doesn't just pop out from the safety of her shadows. There was no "Ta-dahhh! Look at me! I'm out here and loving it!"

(Just like that, we're having a Kramer moment. "I'm out there, Jerry, and I'm lovin' every minute of it!")

Nope. She has learned what happens when she shows her face. The little girl was shut down and shut up over and over again. She was shamed. She was silenced. And she was seen as a trouble maker. Hiding seemed like a much better option.

I didn't trust my own thoughts. They hadn't been freely expressed in years. Giving them a path to be seen and heard out in the open just felt totally foreign. That little girl wasn't just hiding inside of me, she was lost.

So, I had to forge new paths in my mind to help her find a safe way out of the dark.

For me, that meant therapy. (It still means therapy.) It meant that I needed to journal to release all of the thoughts bumping around in my brain, all the feelings swirling in my gut, and all the memories popping up. No more restrained, restricted silence.

I have had to regularly choose to change my mind. Part of that is loving the little girl over and over again until she feels the freedom to come out of the shadows. So, I have learned to encourage myself, to speak truth to myself, and to speak love to myself.

You can't receive love or goodness until you believe you are worthy of it. That starts with you. It begins with baby steps. But you do have to find the courage to take that first step if you're going to be in charge of your mind.

Your authentic voice probably won't just appear and stay out in the open for all the world to see without practice. Be gentle with yourself. Be kind to yourself. And forgive yourself for hiding.

UNTIL

Until one day ... your kid can't fall asleep for months on end. He's twelve. And he can't relax enough to fall asleep. His stomach hurts. He's afraid.

My son couldn't sleep. My kid was scared. Every night.

My gut told me it was anxiety.

I *knew* it was anxiety.

Now, remember he's twelve. So, this kid is getting an attitude. He is in full-on adolescence mode. The hormones. The darn puberty hormones were taking over.

But it's not just puberty. The kid is smart. He's getting smarter by the day and he isn't just book smart. He is emotionally intelligent. And his memory is loooong. As an added bonus, seeing through bullshit is his super power.

He hasn't forgotten a single broken promise, thrown plate, or broken chair. He remembers being lectured in the middle of the night, sixteen whacks with a belt done in secret, being accused without listening, and all of the name calling.

At thirteen, my son was over it. He was done pretending to believe every word from his father's mouth. At thirteen, he was done being accused and accosted verbally and physically in the name of godly discipline.

He could see the game and he refused to play any more.

As you might've guessed, this didn't go over too well with the gaslighter. It turned conflict into explosive encounters that always ended in my son being grounded for weeks and weeks.

As the conflicts escalated, I would position myself within eyeshot and motion for my child to shut his mouth. I silently begged him to stop talking. With every single word of defiance, his dad added another consequence.

To be clear, every single adult who knew my child very well would have described him as a great kid, smart, and respectful. Other parents even told me that he helped their kids make better choices.

At home, a switch flipped. Being forced to go into his room and listen to another lecture did not go well. His dad was determined to put the mouthy thirteen year old in his place. But the boy wasn't having it. He wasn't buying what his dad was selling.

I would watch as his dad would get in his face and call him names. My young boy dug in his heels, lifted his chin in defiance, stared back into the face of fury, and said, "You're a jerk."

Terror struck my heart. *What the hell is he doing? Shut up. Shut. Up.*

Nope. That kid was truly done. He refused to pretend that his dad's word was supreme. He refused to show respect in the face of blind rage and repeated accusations.

I tried to step in ... I cannot come close to counting the number of times I followed upstairs and tried different tactics to put a lid on his dad's rage. Again and again, he shut that door in my face. If I did manage to get into the room, I became the reason for his rage escalating.

I was not protecting my own child. I was just shutting up and hoping to not make it worse. So, I'd clean the kitchen, put away laundry, clean the bathrooms, and tell my other kids to put away all of their toys and clothes. Anything that would keep his rage from growing.

Until ... That night.

That night when my eyes were opened and I finally said, *No more.*

I had listened to his critical, shaming comments. I had endured the name-calling, the ever-evolving measuring stick, the unwinnable games, the crazy-making, the thrown dishes, the fists slamming through things, being put against the wall, raging in my face until the spit flies out.

I was surviving.

But that night he picked the wrong target. That night, he picked a thirteen-year-old boy.

I prayed on the edge of my bed as I heard his voice get louder and louder. I begged God to do something. And when I heard the loud bangs and the sound of somebody climbing my son's loft bed ... He did do something.

He sent me racing into that bedroom. As I rushed the door, I could hear my son's petrified screams. "GET OFF ME! GET OFF ME!"

I opened the door to find my child pinned down by his father ... and that is when my own switch was finally flipped. Finally. MY voice came.

I screamed and screamed for him to get down.

Take a wild guess what he did. Seriously, guess.

He got down ...

And then he looked at me like I was crazy.

"You're insane," he told me and explained how I had no clue what our son was saying to him.

For once, I was not having it. I was listening to none of his reasoning and excuses. I could clearly see the lines he was crossing. I refused to accept his words. I refused to own his thoughts and feelings.

Why had it taken the unmistakable abuse of my own child to wake me up?

WAKING UP

Yep. I was awake.

Of course I was awake. I certainly wasn't sleeping. Who can sleep when your world has completely imploded?

My first phone call the morning after walking out was to a therapist. I sobbed and blubbered my story.

"I have been doing this for a long time. I don't want to scare you, but this is the worst case of emotional abuse I have ever heard," he told me. He went on to use the words "spiritual abuse" and "gaslighting."

I didn't know what to do with those words … but then he sent me a text describing how gaslighting works.

Woah. That was the first time a trained professional could see my situation for what it was. It wasn't friends. It wasn't family. It was someone who was specifically trained to recognize relational issues.

> "Look at how a single candle can both defy and
> define the darkness."
>
> —Anne Frank

I had been living in darkness. My darkness was only afforded the light as he allowed. He had been directing what I was and wasn't allowed to see, what was and wasn't acceptable for illumination.

He was deciding for *all of us*.

He silenced my voice and shut down my choices … and then blamed me for the darkness.

Waking up is not easy. Naming your abuse is not easy. Realizing you have been the sucker of a gaslighter is hard to comprehend.

I am a smart person. I am a discerning person. Other women seek my counsel. And yet, I had been completely fooled for years and years.

It wasn't until I watched my children suffer mentally, emotionally, and physically that I began to see his behavior for what it was—*abusive*. But I couldn't say it out loud. I couldn't own it.

I did not want this story for my life. I begged God in prayer after prayer to keep this exact crap from being part of my story. I begged God to keep pages like this out of my children's life story.

Sometimes God says no.
Sometimes God doesn't send anyone to rescue you.
Sometimes God leaves you in your closet of despair.

It feels wrong. It feels lonely. It feels hopeless. And it feels completely impossible.

Waking up means walking away. Waking up means walking back *to yourself*.

Gaslighting is abusive. True gaslighting is pervasive. It isn't a one-time occurrence in a moment of weakness, anger, or hurt. Gaslighting is an abuser's way of life. It's meant to keep you in the darkness. It's meant to keep you mentally scrambling and confused.

You are not supposed to recognize it. You are supposed to believe that *you* are the problem.

Are you the problem? Well, are you? Do other people in your life see you the same way that he sees you?

I want you to answer. In the back of your mind what whispers are you hearing?

I can tell you that it took months and months of therapy for me to stop questioning whether I was the narcissist. My therapist would catch me contemplating it (without actually saying it outloud) and call me out. "You are not a narcissist."

So, seriously. Make a list of the people who love you that see you the same way your abuser does. I'm guessing nobody who makes you feel loved is on that list.

If there are several people on your list and any of them took care of you as a child, sweet love, please find someone to help you. Find a counselor. Find someone who is a trained therapist to help you wade through the depths of your wounds.

When the people in your life truly see you, they don't gaslight you. The people who truly see you embrace you as you wake up and take an honest look at your reality. Those people believe you. They tell you you're not crazy.

You are not crazy.

Gaslighting puts you in a crazymaking cycle. It is meant to make you feel crazy.
Gaslighting robs you of your power. It is meant to make you feel powerless.
Gaslighting lies to you. It is meant to make you see lies as truth.

But.
You are sane.
You have power.
You know the truth.

When you wake up, you have choices.

You can choose to take back your power. Nobody gets to keep your power. I mean *nobody*. Your power belongs to you and only you.

You can choose to tell the truth. You want your children to tell the truth, right? You've been teaching them to pretend they don't know the truth. But when you wake up, it's time for the truth to kiss its hiding place goodbye.

You can choose to believe yourself. You don't need to question your memory or your gut. The feeling in your gut that you learned to ignore has a purpose and you can choose to pay attention to it.

You can choose to find your voice. You have been silent for too long. Your voice is still there, it's waiting to be found by you. You've forgotten what it sounds like. You may not even think you'll recognize it ... But you'll learn to.

You will learn to differentiate between your voice and his. This won't happen quickly. It took three months of consistent therapy before I could form sentences that were not filtered through his voice in my head.

If you've been in a long-term relationship with a covert passive-aggressive narcissist, then it may be an especially tedious process. Life with a gaslighting narcissist is like being brainwashed.

Coming out of a relationship with a covert passive-aggressive narcissist is like walking away from a cult. Your thinking has been deeply affected.

It took weeks for me to admit *out loud* that I had been abused. I just couldn't say it. I did not want to admit it. My mouth could not form the words. No joke. And the shame was lurking around me ...

What does that say about me?
What kind of person stays in an abusive marriage?
What kind of mother keeps her children in that environment?
What kind of woman chooses a man who treats her this way?

But.

I had choices. I *have* choices. I can choose to remember who I am. I can choose to remember the woman buried underneath the lies. I can choose who I will become. *Me.* I choose that.

You can choose. *You can.* If you have this book, then your life is clearly not over. You're still breathing, right? That's *your* breath. Whose air will you breathe in? It's time for you to choose to wake up and stay awake.

STAY AWAKE

When you wake up, you have to stay awake. Don't allow yourself to be lulled back into the web you just escaped from.

It is so sooo easy to find yourself right back in a gaslighter's web. And you won't even know it's happening until after you're stuck there, paralyzed. Deer in the freaking headlights.

Until …

You remember where you are. You see the trap for what it is. And you make your way out of it. There is no reason for you to remain stuck when you recognize where you are.

But you have to stay awake to stay out of the trap. I'm not kidding. You literally have to be on high alert so you can see the interactions for what they are—gaslighting. Yesss. The gaslighting does not stop after you wake up.

You are not the only person who has experienced gaslighting from your abuser. (Yep. I am going to keep saying "your abuser." Make it part of your vocabulary!) He's good at it, really good. His words sound so noble, so insightful … so full of crap. Do NOT eat his crap.

And if you have kids, they're hearing it, too. Guess what? Your kids are not only being gaslighted, they are learning to gaslight, and seeds are probably being planted to believe that their mom is a little crazy, in a dark place, not following the Lord, the cause of all this yuck.

If you want to stay awake, then you need to be prepared to work. I don't mean get a job and take care of your family. I mean be prepared to work on yourself. If you won't take the time to work on yourself, then you are going to find yourself walking in the same shoes over and over and over.

Same shoes = same path.

Do you want to keep walking this road you've been on? NO. No you don't. You want a different life. You need a different life.

It's time to find your voice. And it's time to find people who will do that with you. When you've lived with a gaslighter, you've lived with trauma. Trauma needs to be acknowledged and healed.

You deserve to heal. Do you hear me? *You deserve to heal.*

Without acknowledging your trauma and facing it, you cannot move forward. You will be stuck and you will find yourself in another destructive relationship. And haven't you lived through enough destruction?

You cannot remain awake without working on yourself consistently. This is not a church-on-Christmas kinda healing. This is a daily walk. It is a commitment you make to yourself. It's a commitment you make to your children.

And it's a commitment you ask of those you know and trust.

Maybe you don't have a support system. Maybe you feel completely alone. If this is you, I feel this. Boy, do I feel this. You've endured a relationship in emotional isolation. You've probably pushed people away.

You can tell the truth. It's time.

But don't expect your abuser to tell the truth. Set the expectation right now that your abuser will lie. Your abuser will lie to your long-time friends, your family, his family, your neighbors, your church leaders, and he will lie to his children. Yes, he will lie to his children about their mother.

Here's the thing. Abusers need therapy. They need to be seen by someone who is not emotionally affected by anything they say. They need somebody who can see through smokescreens. But most of them won't go.

People may tell you repeatedly that leaving the house will open their eyes. People will tell you that filing for separation will surely open their eyes. And people will be certain that filing for divorce will definitely open their eyes and make them finally see what they're doing.

Umm ... maybe. This does happen for some people. You cannot bank on this. You can pray and you can hope, but you must also be wise and discerning as you separate yourself from the situation and look at your abuser's consistent behavior without emotion. Pay attention to your gut.

You got used to that feeling that swirls down in the pit of your stomach. Now it's time to see it for what it really is: a red flag. Your body is trying to tell you, "Danger, Will Robinson! Danger!"

Remember. Gaslighting abusers do not live in reality, they retell their stories to fit the narrative that works for them. Their narratives are clever, they are gut-wrenching, and they are designed to make them out as the victim while you are the dangerous, lying, abusive person.

Their fingers will always be at the ready to point blame at you. They are trigger happy. And you are the perfect target to trigger.

Expect to be triggered. It's going to happen. Your body will react faster than your mind. So mentally prepare yourself. You're trying to reconnect to your brain without his voice running interference.

Staying awake means that you live with your eyes wide open to the truth of your gaslighter. You can no longer lie to yourself or anybody else.

Embrace the mess.
Embrace the hurt.
Embrace the truth.

And move forward.

WALK ON

Reach out to churches and ask for counseling resources. You may have to call a few until somebody gets it. Reach out to women's shelters and tell them you need therapy. Look for ministries in your area that help families in need. All of these people have resources.

And, believe it or not, there are going to be resources on social media. Search Facebook for single parent groups. Solo Parent Society is a fantastic national group of parents who are parenting kiddos alone. Many of these parents have endured major abuse at the hands of their former spouses.

You can do this. You can move forward.

Will you feel like you're wading through tar? Maybe.
Will you experience panic attacks? That's a real possibility.
Will you cry yourself to sleep? More than likely.
Will you find yourself missing the abuser? Probably.

I had no idea that I was suffering from anxiety and PTSD until I saw him again. Crying uncontrollably as my heart raced in the parking lot before sitting in the same room was a pretty good clue. It wasn't until I doubled over sobbing and began to hyperventilate that I realized how horrible a panic attack feels.

(Just typing these words has made my jaw clench together and my teeth grind. And there is nobody in the room with me other than my pups.)

Your body knows danger. So, when your mind cannot settle and your thoughts are scrambled, close your eyes and allow yourself to listen to your body. Consider your circumstances and pay attention to what is triggering you.

Now you can evaluate that trigger. Write it down … what happened, how you responded, what you were thinking, how your stomach felt, how your neck felt, how your shoulders felt, or how your jaw felt. And talk to somebody about it.

You are not meant to live in darkness. Secrets live in shadows. Fear grows in hidden places. Walk on, step out into the light.

And know this: He will more than likely continue to use his same old tactics. He will use the same tried and true phrases that trigger you. He will employ the same body language and facial expressions. Your abuser will use anything he can to convince you that everything is your fault, you are crazy, you are sinful and wicked, and you need to change.

He's right. You do need to change. But not for him, never for him. *Never ever again for him.* You need to change so that you can walk on without his thumb on you.

That thumb holding you down is an illusion. Don't buy into it any more. You are free. Remind yourself that *you are free.*

Will you backslide after making tons of progress? Ehh, probably. Will you get frustrated when your body reacts more quickly than your mind sending your heartbeat into overdrive? Yep.

But that's okay. *It is.*

You don't want to live in a place of fear with your heart racing and your stomach in knots. Nobody does. So, you'll need to focus on doing the work to retrain your mind. Your abuser turned your thought pathways into a maze that he controlled.

You are not in the maze. No matter how much your body might get tense and make you think you're still there, you are not. You have walked on. You can see your way out.

So, slow down. Think about what is true. And walk the hell on.

NOW WHAT?

If you think you can walk away and he won't try to get you back, think again. A gaslighter will apologize. Your abuser will tell you they're sorry.

Ohhh, they're sorry alright. They are sorry that they no longer have you around to make their life work. They are sorry that they can no longer control you. And they are very sorry that the reality you have helped to build is missing its supporting actress.

Keep your distance. And at all costs, **avoid verbal interaction**. Talking to you is a gaslighter's sweet spot. Engaging them in conversation is futile. You know this.

You know that conversations with him have only one winner, and it is never you. Every conversation is like stepping onto a battlefield. Do not engage. I repeat. **Do not engage.**

He is no longer in control. Guess who has control now? You do. And that is unacceptable. He wants it back.

Don't give him control.

Every opportunity to talk with you is an opportunity to charm you, to woo you, to lull you into a false sense of security, and to engage in a conversation that makes you question reality. Every conversation is a new opportunity to gaslight you! So no matter how tempted you are, don't do it.

Stick with texts and emails. And allow yourself a chance to think before you respond. Yes, respond. Do not react. Take all the emotion out of your responses and refuse to let your feelings lead you. When you are reactionary, you're giving up control.

He is going to trigger you. You can bet on that. Triggers will make you feel like you are out of control, that's a lie. You're just triggered. Plain and simple.

Until you give up control, it's still in your hands. Think of your control as part of your power. You are allowed to have power. Hold onto your power as though your life depends on it ... because it does. When he has control, he has your quality of life in his hands.

Your abuser's hands are not trustworthy. Do not let him hold your heart or your mind hostage.

Listen, I am very aware that you have been biting your tongue for what may very well feel like an eternity. While you were still in the relationship with your abuser, you bit your tongue and stayed silent to survive.

Your feelings were probably disregarded, so you learned to keep them to yourself. Now that you are no longer sharing a bed, you may want to unbridle your tongue and finally be honest.

He unbridles his tongue whenever he wants and rationalizes every hateful word. Now it's your turn. And you have been waiting a long dern time to have your turn. Your sister has told you to unleash. Your mom has given you full permission to go full-throttle.

Sorry, but no.

Yeah … hard pass.

Don't do that. **Do NOT let go of your tongue.** Your feelings and thoughts are precious. They are coming from a wounded place deep inside of you. And he cannot have them. It's not time for you to share that piece of yourself with someone who has taken so much.

And it won't make you feel better. It will add fuel to his fire and fan the flames of his rage and ridiculous rationalizations. He will turn your words into weapons to use against you. Do not give him the satisfaction.

You absolutely must guard your words. They are not safe with him. In your attempt to wound him or put him in his place, you may find yourself on the receiving end of a condescending, vicious verbal attack full of reasons why you deserve to receive what he has to say to you.

This is the time for you to heal, find your voice, and get your feet firmly under you. You cannot do that with his voice regularly trying to re-root itself in your head. You cannot move forward because verbal or in-person contact is like taking the lines of your freshly rewritten emotional script and erasing them.

Your abuser, your gaslighter, does not want you to think without him. Never forget that. He wants you to believe that you need him to make the right decisions. Gaslighters do not want you to have confidence in yourself.

But …

What do *you* want?

That question may not be easy to answer. It may take you a while to know what it is that you want. And until you do, it is nobody else's job to decide for you. Your decision-making process has been taken away from you for a long time.

Take it back and *keep it.*

Start small. Make your own decisions about groceries, what you'll eat, what you'll wear. Every single time you make a choice without validation or input from another person, congratulate yourself!

You ARE of Sound Mind!

This is not my soapbox to stand and preach at you about being in control and having power. That is not what I mean by any of this. I mean take control of your mind. If you are a believer, then you know that you have been given a sound mind.

You do not need another person to do your thinking and make your decisions. It may take you longer to make decisions for a while as you grow in your confidence. Remind yourself regularly that you are capable of controlling yourself. You can't control others, but you can control your*self.*

And this is the perfect time to journal. It's a completely safe way for you to be 100% messy with your thoughts. It's also a great way to gauge your progress. You can look back and see how far you've come.

Did you just roll your eyes? Wellll … I'm serious. It helps to write down all the overwhelming things on paper. It just gets them out of the dark places where they're hiding. You can write affirmations about yourself, acknowledge lies you believe, and envision a future, more confident version of your true self.

You can do this. I will keep telling you because it's true. Until you believe it for yourself, you need people who will remind you that *you are* capable.

My First Weeks

I want to have this story of walking away and driving straight into a beautiful sunset, that my kids were relieved and happy, and that all the pieces just fell into place.

But my kids watched me cry alone and fall apart.

We had nowhere to go. We had no clothes. We had none of our regular "stuff." My mind was racing. My emotions were all over the place. I could barely think straight, let alone come up with a plan.

I didn't want to get gas with my checkcard because I knew he would be watching the bank account like a hawk to see where we were and what I was doing. I was on the phone with friends, pastors, church counselors, and so many family members.

I'd made sure to keep them all in the dark—just like any well-trained abuse victim.

Enter in all the people who began praying for a miracle. There were so many people convinced that he just needed to "wake up" so he could change. After all, he was a Christian. Surely he'd feel some conviction about what happened.

That's absolutely not what happened.

He was texting constantly, telling me that I shouldn't have left and that I was making things worse. He wasn't remorseful. He was pissed. And I didn't answer a single text.

Someone gave me money to go to Walmart so I could buy clothes and supplies for us because we were all wearing the same clothes. We didn't have socks, underwear, toothbrushes, or toys for the kids.

I was actually afraid to run any errands because I didn't want him to see my car anywhere, and I definitely didn't want to run into him. Imagine the feeling of your jaw being clenched, but it's your entire body. Now add a dash of trembling.

Meanwhile, we are staying in another house. That makes a second set of beds for me and the kids to sleep in. A second set of people for us to be with. And we all knew it was only temporary.

In the next two months, we'd stay at several places. I would wake up at 2:30 a.m. to clean buildings until 6:00 a.m. Most of those nights, I barely slept before going into work because my mind wouldn't shut off. So, I would finish work and go back to sleep.

All the while, I was barely functioning. I had no emotional or mental energy to give to my kids. I cried nearly every time I was alone. Often, I was sobbing because I felt so guilty for taking the kids away from their father and I knew he missed them.

I was a wreck. And I couldn't *not* be a wreck.

Some people around me were preaching reconciliation while others were hoping for divorce. I was nowhere near being ready to use the word divorce.

Then the messages and calls start happening. People were reaching out to tell me just how awful divorce would be and that I just didn't know the ramifications of choosing divorce. I listened to multiple lessons from women with whom he had shared his version of the story.

I wasn't even using the word divorce with anybody—not my family, not my friends. And people who actually knew my story would never have called to tell me what happens when people get divorced. They would have known that I didn't want my kids to experience the same pain I did as a child.

In the meantime, I was going to therapy weekly. I was very slowly coming face to face with my reality. Abuse was no longer a foreign concept, it was an intimate one. And my voice was making its way out of the shadows.

I was begging God to be with me. As I lay in bed at night, I would ask him to wrap his arms around me and comfort me. I was exhausted mentally, emotionally, and physically, but I couldn't sleep through the night.

I woke up with my mind racing multiple times a night for months. All the anxiety that I had been living with for the past twenty years finally felt the freedom to show up. It showed up in a racing heart, tight chest, shallow breaths, foggy brain, bursts of anger, and panic attacks.

"You have PTS and anxiety," my therapist told me. I had no idea you could develop post traumatic stress from emotional and mental trauma. The truth is that trauma from pro-longed exposure to emotional and mental trauma is more invasive that physical abuse.

The unseen abuse leaves its mark so deeply that it affects your genes. The only way to heal these trauma markers on your genes is through therapy. Lots and lots of therapy.

I walked my butt straight into therapy. I slobbered and snotted my way through it. I have no idea what I said in those first weeks. My sentences were jumbled and unfinished. My feelings were all over the place.

Until one day they weren't. One day, I wasn't full of mental and emotional tangles. I could take a breath without my chest tightening around my lungs and stifling me. I could picture a future that I liked.

It took a solid eighteen months of therapy before I could even entertain the thought of being near a man. Before that, I would tense up at the idea of a man holding my hand, much less going on a date. And it was another year of therapy before my therapist said I was ready to date.

Managing kids, getting therapy, finding places to live, handling my kids' anxieties, changing schools, working for myself full time, and trying to pay all of our bills has been a lot. *A lot a lot.*

I've cried. I've screamed. I've curled up in a ball. I've lost my temper. I've lost my marbles.

And I've found myself.

I've found my identity. I've found my voice. I've found *me.*

Please do not hear me saying I have been on a self-involved journey of this buzzword-worthy self-discovery mumbo jumbo. This is not that. This is not a do-whatever-makes-you-happy journey.

Traveling to a tropical island would make me happy. Going to Greece would make me happy. Straightening my teeth, erasing my wrinkles, and getting a tummy tuck would make me happy.

This. Is. Not. That.

You don't really get to the core of who you are by escaping or "fixing" your outsides. Would I like to do those things? Umm, you betcha. But I wouldn't have done any internal work to get them. And I sure as Sheila wouldn't be helping my kids heal or setting an example for them.

This is setting myself up for better decisions, better relationships, better emotional and mental health.

This is learning how and why I stayed in a toxic relationship so that I never do it again.

This is paying attention to my children so they learn what it looks like to live in thrive mode rather than survival mode.

This is navigating my past so it doesn't dictate my present or my future.

This is embracing both my past and my present without shame.

This is not living for self. This is loving self.

You are worth every single baby step it takes to move out of the shadows so you can feel the warmth of love and embrace of hope.

You may feel abandoned. You may feel unprotected. You may feel terrified. Your feelings are real and valid. It is okay to feel all of those things. But please, give yourself grace. Give yourself the gift of healing.

Healing alone keeps you where he had you. Healing alone is almost a contradiction in terms because you need another voice or ten to speak to your wounded soul. Isolation is familiar, but it is not your friend.

Get online. Look for Celebrate Recovery and CoDA near you. Start with those things. And if you haven't walked away, go to the library and look these up so you're not afraid of him seeing your search history. Do some research on intimate partner violence and look for a list of therapists who know how to treat it.

There are resources for you to get your head above water. So, fight for yourself. Fight for this moment. Fight for this day. And when you wake up tomorrow, do it again, knowing that you only need enough strength to make it through the now.

An enemy is coming for you. He is cunning. He is crafty. And he knows every single weakness, every button you have. He will play on your heartache and insecurity. He will hit you again and again telling you that you can't do it.

But you have done it. You are here. You are breathing. You are not defeated.

You are worth more than the lies planted in your mind. Don't water them. Don't give them light. Take back your light and shine it on the truth living inside of you.

Satan came to steal, kill, and destroy. But Jesus came to give you a full life. (John 10:10) I can say with full confidence that I have had more than enough stolen from me. So have you.

Even today, I cried. I cried because my circumstances overwhelmed me. I cried because I'm lonely. I cried because I want financial freedom.

But you know what? I didn't cry because I feel like a piece of crap. I didn't cry because I feel trapped. I didn't cry because I don't feel loved.

I am free to cry. I am free to have every single feeling. And I am free to hope.

Lucky me.

BELIEVE

*"You never change things by fighting the existing reality.
To change something, build a new model that makes the existing model obsolete."*

—Buckminster Fuller

You have been abused. Yep. I said it. It is what it is. It is part of your story. It's part of my story. And it is a part we cannot erase.

We don't have to like it. But we do need to own it. To admit it. To accept it. And to stop denying it. Until we do that, we cannot move forward.

You may move on. You may create space. But you won't move forward. You may be in a different space physically. That's good. Keep that space between you. Keeping your distance is wise.

Until you stop fighting the truth, you will not be able to walk forward in truth.

Walking forward in truth will move you into a different place mentally and emotionally. That is what you need. You don't need to pretend it didn't happen. You don't need to ignore it. You don't need to lie to yourself about it.

You need to believe in the person that you are *and* the person you are becoming.

Gaslighters silence the voice of their victims. Gaslighters rob their victims of truth. Gaslighters take a victim's power and dominate it with their own.

Gaslighters will dictate truth to you.

If you let them.

And they will continue to define all the truth in your life and the lives of your children as long as they are allowed to do it.

So, will you?

Will you let your abuser's voice continue to speak with more authority over your life than your own?

Will you let your abuser decide what you think?

Will you let your abuser tell the rest of your story?

OR

Will you choose to believe that *you* are worth fighting for? That your heart and your mind are worth fighting for?

Believe it.

You can walk away, walk on, and walk into a reality that is between you and God.

Finally …

Lucky you.

AFTERWORD

It took me a solid year to go back and re-read the words on these pages. And you know what? I still cried. I still feel terrible about what my kids suffered. I am still horrified at the abuse I lived with on a regular basis.

But now, in some ways, I feel as if I'm reading about another person. That girl was scared all the time. That girl was ashamed of her upbringing. That girl was emotionally and mentally isolated.

That's not who I am anymore.

Did life get incredibly hard for me financially? Have I been physically exhausted? Umm. Absolutely.

But. I do not live in fear of another human under my own roof. I know my voice. I know my own mind. I am free.

I want every person living with the abuse from a covert passive-aggressive narcissist to recognize it, name it, and get out from under the reigning tyranny it's held over their minds.

So, today I can see my abuser without having a panic attack. I can be at my kids' activities without my heart racing out of my chest when he is there. But he still makes me nervous.

And that is okay. I don't let it rule over me. I recognize it for what it is—a warning. My body still remembers the trauma. My body senses the danger. That's exactly what it should do.

I no longer ignore the voice inside me. My voice matters.

And so does yours.

RESOURCES FOR YOU

www.psychologytoday.com/us/therapists/domestic-abuse

www.celebraterecovery.com

coda.org

National Domestic Violence Hotline: 800-799-7233
1-800-787-3224 (TTY)

National Center for Victims of Crime
1-855-4-VICTIM (1-855-484-2846)

If you are experiencing **intimate partner violence**. It is abuse. According to the American Psychological Association, intimate partner violence is defined as follows:

"physical, psychological, or sexual abuse of one person by another in a close relationship. The couple may be heterosexual or same-sex, and they may be (or have been) dating, married, or living together. Apart from violence and threats of abuse, control is a hallmark of the abusive intimate partner relationship, with the aggressor controlling the partner's access to family and friends, taking control of shared finances, and constantly monitoring the partner's activities. If rejected, the perpetrator may also stalk the partner. Victims of intimate partner violence are at greater risk for developing depression, substance abuse, and other disorders."

The Department of Justice considers intimate partner violence to be domestic violence. According to their website this is Domestic Violence:

"Domestic violence is a pattern of abusive behavior in any relationship that is used by one partner to gain or maintain power and control over another intimate partner. Domestic violence can be physical, sexual, emotional, economic, psychological, or technological actions or threats of actions or other patterns of coercive behavior that influence another person within an intimate partner relationship. This includes any behaviors that intimidate, manipulate, humiliate, isolate, frighten, terrorize, coerce, threaten, blame, hurt, injure, or wound someone. Examples of abusive behavior include:

"Physical Abuse: Hitting, slapping, shoving, grabbing, pinching, biting, hair pulling, etc. are types of physical abuse. This type of abuse also includes denying a partner medical care or forcing alcohol and/or drug use upon him or her.

"Sexual Abuse: Coercing or attempting to coerce any sexual contact or behavior without consent. Sexual abuse includes, but is certainly not limited to, marital rape, attacks on sexual parts of the body, forcing sex after physical violence has occurred, or treating one in a sexually demeaning manner.

"Emotional Abuse: Undermining an individual's sense of self-worth and/or self-esteem is abusive. This may include, but is not limited to constant criticism, diminishing one's abilities, name-calling, or damaging one's relationship with his or her children.

"**Economic Abuse:** Controlling or restraining a person's ability to acquire, use, or maintain economic resources to which they are entitled. This includes using coercion, fraud, or manipulation to restrict a person's access to money, assets, credit, or financial information; unfairly using a person's personal economic resources, including money, assets, and credit, or exerting undue influence over a person's financial and economic behavior or decisions, including forcing default on joint or other financial obligations, exploiting powers of attorney, guardianship, or conservatorship, or failing or neglecting to act in the best interests of a person to whom one has a fiduciary duty.

"**Psychological Abuse:** Elements of psychological abuse include - but are not limited to - causing fear by intimidation; threatening physical harm to self, partner, children, or partner's family or friends; destruction of pets and property; and forcing isolation from family, friends, or school and/or work.

"**Technological Abuse:** An act or pattern of behavior that is intended to harm, threaten, control, stalk, harass, impersonate, exploit, extort, or monitor another person that occurs using any form of technology, including but not limited to: internet enabled devices, online spaces and platforms, computers, mobile devices, cameras and imaging programs, apps, location tracking devices, or communication technologies, or any other emerging technologies.

"Domestic violence can happen to anyone regardless of race, age, sexual orientation, religion, sex, or gender identity. Domestic violence affects people of all socioeconomic backgrounds and education levels. Domestic violence occurs in both opposite-sex and same-sex relationships and can happen to intimate partners who are married, living together, dating, or share a child.

"Domestic violence not only affects those who are abused, but also has a substantial effect on family members, friends, co-workers, other witnesses, and the community at large. Children, who grow up witnessing domestic violence, are among those seriously affected by this crime. Frequent exposure to violence in the home not only predisposes children to numerous social and physical problems, but also teaches them that violence is a normal way of life - therefore, increasing their risk of becoming society's next generation of victims and abusers.

"The discussion here does not alter the definition in VAWA."

Sources: National Domestic Violence Hotline, National Center for Victims of Crime, and WomensLaw.org.

I would also personally add one more type of intimate partner violence.

Spiritual Abuse is a means of targeting a person's predilection to follow God's Word, mature in their faith, and lead others within the church. Each of these things can be used as leverage by an abuser. The abuser picks and chooses verses from the Bible to manipulate their partner with shame, guilt, and accusation.

Spiritual abuse is almost tabu. People in the church shy away from it. But that doesn't make it less real or any less abusive. The Bible is not to be used as a tool for beating others down, a thing to hide behind, or as a source of justification for controlling behavior.

God's word is freedom, not a prison.

ABOUT THE AUTHOR

Tori Wagner spent nearly twenty-five years in a relationship with a covert narcissist. Since freeing herself from it, she has poured her heart, soul, and mind into recovery, healing, and helping other women along the way.

She spends her days with words and her evenings with her kids ... when they're not occupied with some sort of teenagery activity. She loves Jesus, worship music, her kids' playlists in the car, sports, all sorts of really great books, watching superhero movies, BBC television, home-made cake, long hugs, and Christmas morning breakfast with her kids.

Tori has led countless small groups of women in Bible studies and mom groups. You can count on her to show up and help you prep for a party. And you never have to ask her twice to join you on the dance floor.

In between all the heartbeats of her life, Tori is working toward the vision and calling on her life to build a safe haven for women and children who are victims of intimate partner violence.

www.ingramcontent.com/pod-product-compliance
Lightning Source LLC
LaVergne TN
LVHW011249290425
809785LV00008B/110